MANAGEMENT AND MORALE

MANAGEMENT AND MORALE

BY

F. J. ROETHLISBERGER

Professor of Human Relations, Graduate School of Business Administration, Harvard University

HARVARD UNIVERSITY PRESS
CAMBRIDGE, MASSACHUSETTS
AND LONDON, ENGLAND

Seventeenth Printing, 1975

LIBRARY OF CONGRESS CATALOG CARD NUMBER 41–4302

ISBN 0–674–54650–4

PRINTED IN THE UNITED STATES OF AMERICA

To

PHILIP CABOT

WHOSE INTEREST IN THINKING SCIENTIFICALLY HAS NOT DIMINISHED HIS CAPACITY FOR ACTING INTELLIGENTLY

ACKNOWLEDGMENTS

THE IDEAS presented in this book are the product of a collaborative research effort rather than the work of any one person. Particularly is this true of the point of view regarding the nature and treatment of coöperative phenomena. As a member of a research group for the past fifteen years, I find it difficult to state accurately or specifically the contribution each person has made to my thinking.

For the opportunity to become immersed in concrete data and to obtain a firsthand acquaintance with the facts of human association before theorizing about them, I am greatly indebted to Professor Elton Mayo. To him I owe my clinical orientation as well as my understanding of the structure of obsessive thinking. To Dr. L. J. Henderson special mention should also be given. The occasional footnotes testify only in part to the great use I have made of his systematic statements on some of the most difficult problems relating to the conceptual treatment of coöperative phenomena.

Sincere appreciation is also due to former colleagues with whom at various periods I was closely associated, and who helped to formulate my thinking. These include Dr. Conrad M. Arensberg, Dr. Eliot D. Chapple, Dr. Burleigh Gardner, Mr. Sargent Kennedy, Mr. O. S. Lovekin, Dr. Hans Molholm, Dr. Paul Pigors, Professor W. Lloyd Warner, and Professor T. North Whitehead.

I owe much to the Hawthorne Works of the Western Electric Company, in whose researches on employee relations I had the unusual opportunity of participating. From my association with those intimately concerned with these researches — Mark L. Putnam, Harold A. Wright, William J. Dickson, and Arthur C. Moore — I learned a great deal about the human problems of industrial organization. In particular, my indebtedness to William J. Dickson is great. We spent several arduous and happy years in reducing these researches to words on paper. Inasmuch as several of the chapters in this book were written during the period after the first rough draft of the Hawthorne researches had been completed in 1936, but before their publication in 1939, they still bear the indelible stamp of this joint authorship.

For the daily human satisfactions, encouragement, support, and stimulation they provided, the members of the present research group deserve my highest appreciation. The material used in some of the chapters came from two recent researches in which I was closely associated with John B. Fox and George F. F. Lombard. Also, Dr. B. M. Selekman, Dr. F. L. W. Richardson, Jr., George C. Homans, Gordon T. Bowden, and Dr. John C. Cooley deserve mention.

Among recent influences on my thinking, Mr. Chester I. Barnard's statements on the functions of the executive have first place. This will be quite apparent in many of the chapters that follow. The discerning reader will also see signs of the works of Pareto and Korzybski. Recent influences should also include Professors Talcott Parsons and Clyde K. M. Kluckhohn.

A research group interested in the empirical study of the human problems of administration needs close association with those who are dealing with and trying to teach an understanding of the complex problems of business administration; it needs the coöperation of business organizations in order to conduct its studies; it needs an intelligent audience on which it can test its ideas; last, but not least, it needs funds. In all these respects we have been exceedingly fortunate. Our colleagues at the Harvard Graduate School of Business Administration, under the able leadership of Dean Wallace B. Donham, have helped to keep our attention on the practical and complex problems of business, with their emphasis on the "case system" and the study of concrete particular business problems. In conducting our studies we have been fortunate in receiving the coöperation of executives from such business organizations as the American Telephone and Telegraph Company, General Motors Corporation, Hood Rubber Company, Inc., R. H. Macy and Company, Inc., Swift and Company, Western Electric Company, Inc., and Westinghouse Electric and Manufacturing Company. Professor Philip Cabot's Business Executives' Discussion Groups provided a sympathetic and intelligent audience on which to test our ideas. Only by the continued support of the Rockefeller Foundation were these researches possible.

Whatever literary and grammatical merit the book has belongs to Mrs. Hilda Richardson Carter for her skillful and adroit editorial services, which still allow me to retain my pride of authorship. To Miss Elizabeth Brown and Miss Betty Boyle goes the credit for performing effectively and with enthusiasm the many laborious but highly important tasks which accompany the publication of a book.

It is needless to say that the entire responsibility for the statements made in this book is the author's alone.

F. J. R.

July 15, 1941

CONTENTS

FOREWORD

He is an inveterate optimist who is not sobered by a comparison of our own time with the high expectations of a century ago. Bernard Cracroft, writing in 1867, expressed the general attitude of the early years of the nineteenth century. "The mercantile fever," "the ardent faith in progress" were based upon belief in "the boundless development of human energy striving like fire ever upwards." "Unforeseen but probable discoveries" were expected at any moment to "throw additional millions into the lap of human comfort." By such means it was expected that man would raise himself above the possibilities of privation and strife.

This belief expressed certainty of immense future advance in scientific discovery, mechanical invention, the development of economic knowledge, and industrial organization. And this belief has nowhere proved vain: the actual advance in the last century of scientific discovery, mechanical invention, economic knowledge, and organization has surpassed by far anything that Cracroft and his contemporaries could possibly have anticipated. To cross the continent from coast to coast in a few hours of the night by air has become a commonplace. Men talk to each other across three thousand miles of sea without wires or any tangible connection. In no area of activity have nineteenth-century expectations been disappointed: the fulfillment has by far outdone the hope.

But privation and strife have not vanished from the earth. On the contrary, we look out at a world torn by internecine strife that extends more widely and runs deeper than any other instance history can show. The human privation that has followed, and is still to follow, is of similar dimension. All the immense advancement of knowledge has apparently been powerless to prevent a resurgence of the most savage barbarism. Indeed, it often seems as though scientific advancement has served only to implement — to give weapons to — resurgent barbarism.

This leads to a feeling of confusion and pessimism. The word "chaos" creeps into the daily vocabulary. Evidence given before a recent Senate committee showed a tendency to bitter acceptance of chaos as inevitable. But pessimism of this type is too general, too obsessive. It does not pause to ask more precisely where the chaos lies. In the strict sense, it cannot be said to lie in science, or mechanics, or economics, or industrial organization. The work that has been done, and is being done, in these areas, though necessarily limited, is admirable. But, beyond all this, some essential determinant of order in human affairs has been left out of account in two centuries of rapid development.

The writings of economists hint the omission. Sir Arthur Salter, in 1933, in describing the structure of an ordered society, asserted that no such order can be contrived unless backed by "collective determination." Sir George Paish, in a small and recently published essay, *The Defeat of Chaos* (1941), describes, probably admirably, the economic conditions necessary to the achievement of international (and intranational) prosperity and peace. At the beginning and end of his essay, he mentions a "spirit of willing co-operation" as necessary to any such happy issue out of our afflictions. But he does not tell us how this exceedingly important change is to be effected. The human fact that emerges from these or any other studies is that, *while material efficiency has been increasing for two hundred years, the human capacity for working together has in the same period continually diminished.* Of late, the pace of this deterioration seems to have accelerated. This observation is strikingly evident in the international field; it is evident also within any modern society, if the relation between the constituent groups be closely inspected. Discussions in the technical reviews, somewhat grandiloquently entitled "the growth of nationalism" or "collective bargaining as a means of preventing industrial disputes," merely serve to mask the fact that the human capacity for spontaneous coöperation has greatly diminished or, at least, has not kept pace with other development.

This alarming break in the structure of civilization did not appear suddenly in 1939, nor was it first manifest in 1914. For at least a century competent observers, Cassandra-like, have called attention to the danger. At the very time when Cracroft published his *Essays on Reform* (1867), Frederic Le Play was continuously writing up his studies of the European worker made between the years 1829 and 1855. Le Play was a French engineer who, by reason of his professional interest, had traveled widely through the Continent. Believing that he observed a diminishing capacity for working together in industrial and urban communities, he set himself to observe and record systematically the social situation in various parts of Europe. His observations extended from the steppes to the Western Atlantic shores: they are recorded in six volumes published between 1855 and 1879; these volumes are still obtainable and are worthy of closer attention than has yet been given them.

His first volumes describe certain of the simpler communities in Northern and Eastern Europe where agriculture or fishing is the central activity. He finds in such communities peace and stability, a simple faith in, and capacity to live by, the social code (for Le Play this code is that of the Decalogue). In such a community the individual understands every social activity and, in greater or less degree, participates in it. The ties of family and kinship operate to relate every person to every social function: human content and happiness, the power to coöperate spontaneously and effectively, are at a high level. The members of such a community do not work together by reason of any sort of social or legal constraint. The social code and the desires of the individual are practically identical; every individual participates because his strongest wish is to do so.

As Le Play's studies move westwards, the communities become more industrial, more urban; the material standard of living is apparently much higher. In his terminology, some communities are merely "shaken," others are already "disorganized"; with great care he describes both situations. The characteristically modern industrial community, he finds, has lost its capacity for peace and stability; the authority of the social code is ignored; the ties of kinship are no longer binding. In such a situation individuals are unhappy, the desire for change — "novelty" — has become almost passionate and leads to further disorganization. The capacity for spontaneous and effective coöperation with other people has almost disappeared. In this situation three characteristic "abuses" make their appearance. These are: the abuse of riches, the "remote" owner cannot be actually coöperative with those whose activities he directs; the abuse of science and knowledge, the supposedly enlightened academic tends more and more to attack and destroy the very traditions upon which coöperative capacity rests; the abuse of power, the destruction of traditional institutions leads to concentration of power in the central political authority — even when this authority is nominally democratic, the move is necessarily in the direction of dictatorship.

Émile Durkheim and his many associates of the French school of sociology made similar observations of various French communities in the last twenty years of the nineteenth century. Their studies are presented in many volumes of *L'Année Sociologique*. In one study, however, Durkheim turned away from the mere recording of the facts to consider the effect upon individual happiness of modern industrial development. This is his well-known study of suicide, and in it he points out that industrial development has diminished not only our capacity for working together but also the sum of human happiness.

Upon the one hand, he demonstrates that the ancient relationships that formerly trained the individual to association and work with others have collapsed or are collapsing; finally the State is left as the sole organizing activity facing "a disordered dust of individuals." On the other hand, the collapse of traditional disciplines has not freed the individual from constraint; on the contrary, it has deprived him of all values other than the merely material, of all sense of direction in living; it has left him to a loneliness previously unknown in human situations and to great personal unhappiness. This is the source of *anomie,* of that planlessness in living which in one form or other relates itself to the disorganization of the communal life demonstrated by Le Play.

These earlier studies tend naturally enough to look back at the life of a simpler community with regret; they tend inevitably to the conclusion that spontaneity of coöperation cannot be recovered except by reversion to the traditional. This is a road that we cannot travel in these days, even if we were certain of its advisability. But the implication of such opinion does not detract from the value of Le Play's observations or of Durkheim's. The real importance of these studies is the clear demonstration that *collaboration in a society cannot be left to chance.* Historically and traditionally our predecessors worked for it — and succeeded. For at least a century of the most amazing scientific and material progress we have abandoned the effort — by inadvertence, it is true — and we are now reaping the consequences. Every social group must secure for its individual and group membership: —

(a) The satisfaction of economic needs.
(b) The maintenance of coöperation organized in social routines.

Our methods are all pointed at efficiency; none at the maintenance of coöperation. We do know how to devise efficient methods; we do not know how to ensure spontaneity of coöperation — that is, teamwork. The latter problem is far more difficult of solution with us than in a simple or primitive community. In a simple society the extent of change from year to year, or even from century to century, may be relatively small. Traditional methods are therefore brought to a high degree of perfection; almost from birth disciplined collaboration is drilled into the individual. But in these days of rapid and continuous change the whole conception of social discipline must probably be altered. Study of the problem must begin rather as an investigation of human happiness than as an anthropological study of ceremonial participation.

The acceleration of change that has characterized the past half century has been extraordinary. In horse-and-buggy days a well-made vehicle would often outlast two human generations and many generations of horse. In these days the average businessman feels somewhat apologetic if his automobile is five years old. In New England in the last generation, textile mills could count on long runs of gingham — scores of thousands of yards in a year. In these days it seems that there is no demand for gingham or for long runs of any type of cloth. So also with processes: in the tin mills of Western Pennsylvania a generation ago, the chief operators were highly skilled persons with a reputation in the mills and an equivalent social position in the community outside. In these days the skill they possess has been completely superseded, their social position by consequence abolished. More important than product or process, however, is the effect of this incessant change upon the human situation. Before the fateful year 1929, Dr. J. S. Plant called attention to the fact that in a prosperous residential district in Essex County, New Jersey, although the greater number of residents owned their own homes, these same houses tended to change hands every five years.

The appearance of this novel character of the human scene

was first noted by Durkheim in the study specified above (1897). He pointed out that it is only a family that has lived long enough in a district to become identified with it by social tradition and economic function that is a family in the sociological sense. The modern family, which breaks up almost as soon as it is formed — the children moving elsewhere for schooling and still further afield for work — such a family cannot help its members to develop capacity for effective association with other people, it cannot give that sense of personal security that derives from a certainty of belonging to an historic group. It is not only economic activities that desert a district; the local families split up and move in different directions also. In this situation, that training for participation in social life that our predecessors gave their children has dwindled almost to nothing.

Yet the desire for continuous and intimate association in work with others remains a strong, possibly the strongest, human capacity. *It is the modern tragedy that the very strength of this persistent desire makes against rather than for effective coöperation.* This occurs in two ways. The first is shown in the apparent increase of obsessive thinking. This has been studied by Janet, by Freud, and by the whole mental hygiene movement in this country. The so-called maladjustment to which these authorities trace the origin of obsession is a social maladjustment. It expresses the strenuous and ineffective efforts of an unhappy individual to relate himself effectively to other persons, when he has not been trained to such relationships. Realization of his own ineffectiveness leads him to overthink the problem, to press too impatiently for some immediate and miraculous solution, and to collapse into depression when his efforts almost certainly fail.

The other way in which the persistence of an instinct for association shows itself is perhaps even more important. There is no statistic to verify the estimate of a large increase in extreme cases of obsession, though all the authorities believe it. But, even if it is so, the consequent problem is small by comparison with that which arises from the intrusion of obsessive ideas into the thinking of persons essentially normal. For this means that in dealing with the already complex affairs of civilization we are faced with the partial intrusion of another, and a human, complication. The relative isolation of small groups, their constant feeling of insecure tenure, imposes upon such groups an attitude of suspicion or even hostility in their attitude to other groups or, in industry, to management. By this road we drift downwards to what the historians call *stasis*, a disintegration of a community into an infinity of mutually hostile sections. By this road come disintegration, chaos, downfall.

This book by my colleague Roethlisberger is a study of what is, in fact, involved in human collaboration; it is addressed to business executives and, more generally, to the intelligent public. The study, which is developed in some detail, serves to demonstrate that collaboration cannot be left to chance, that by inadvertence we have done exactly this for more than a century, and that it is this neglect more than any other determination which has issued in the present chaos. The solution proposed by Le Play and Durkheim is a voluntary return to a simpler society. That proposed by Hitler and Mussolini is a compulsory return to simplicity coupled with a drastic abolition of academic "intellectualists." Roethlisberger shows that there are other methods, not at any point in conflict with the democratic tradition, that may be applied to the remedy of our social and industrial ills.

ELTON MAYO

July 1, 1941.

PART I

CHAPTER I

INTRODUCTION

THE purpose of this book is to present the application of a point of view to problems of human collaboration with particular reference to the modern industrial scene. It is intended to show that collaboration is not only a subject for exhortation but also a field for serious study and research. Each chapter in Part I was originally an address made to a group of businessmen interested in the field of human relations. Each had more or less the same purpose — to call to their attention a neglected area of consideration regarding problems of human collaboration, as well as to present a point of view which can be simply but effectively practiced in their shops and offices, in factories, retail stores, banks. In this sense each address, regardless of its title, is saying more or less the same thing. However, the central theme is presented each time in a slightly different form. Sometimes, as it were, it is played in the major key, sometimes in the minor key. Sometimes it is even "swung." Each chapter, however, was written in a context which dictated a style of exposition that it was hoped would appeal to and be understood by the businessman.

These addresses were written during the years 1936 to 1941. Roughly, this period coincides with the second term of Roosevelt's administration. To those in the fields of business and labor during this turbulent period, these articles may appear naïve, their examples trivial — all in all, disappointing. Surely with the National Labor Relations Act, the "Baby" Wagner Acts, the Fair Labor Standards Act, and other forms of labor legislation; with lockouts, walkouts, "quickies," sitdowns, and jurisdictional disputes; with heated discussions on "human rights" versus "property rights," and with more learned discussions of the effects of collective bargaining upon wages, employment, the formation of capital, the business cycle, and competition between union and nonunion plants — surely among all these problems, and their intensification with the outbreak of war, there were more important and pressing matters which needed attention and discussion. This possible reaction on the part of some readers will help in defining the purpose of these articles and the point of view which they represent.

Our research group were not entirely unaware of the controversies raging around us in newspapers, magazines, journals, reviews, and books. At lunch, as well as in discussion groups, meetings, lectures, and conferences, we even participated in these verbal controversies; but, for the most part, we preferred to study concrete situations in order to find out why certain people acted, felt, and believed as they did. This attitude of ours at times became quite disconcerting because in the heat of discussion on the "rights of labor" or the "interference of government in business" we often became more interested in the personal and social attitudes of the discussants than in the finely spun logical points of the discussion. Using the point of view which our group had developed, we felt that simple uniformities in human behavior were much more readily discernible — such uniformities as might make that uniformity of uniformities, the so-called law of gravitation in its ordinary and everyday manifestation, blush for shame.

In all these discussions, we felt that tremendous emphasis was being given to the legal, logical, technical, political, and verbal machinery for securing collaboration between people. Hence, something needed to be said to balance this overemphasis. Were not important determinants of effective collaboration being ignored? What evidence was there that collaboration was primarily a matter of logical and legal contrivance? In fact, the evidence on the other side seemed to us so overwhelming that in each talk an attempt was made to point out certain serious omissions in considering the problem of collaboration, as well as to suggest a simple method of taking them into account.

In each address which follows there is a level of discourse that cuts across ideological differences on the subject of labor relations. This level is sometimes dignified by the labels "scientific," "factual," or "objective." There will be no attempt to borrow these dignified words for our popular expositions of a point of view. Each reader, in terms of his own understanding of these terms, can decide for himself whether or not they apply. This much, however, can be said: in each paper an effort was made to limit statements to three different classes.

The first class of statements are statements regarding a useful and convenient way of thinking about a limited class of phenomena—in this case those involving the interactions of two or more people. These statements will express the widest generalizations possible for this class of phenomena. Many of them will appear in abbreviated form. Such statements, for example, as "Business is a social as well as an economic phenomenon," in their complete form would read, "It is useful and convenient to regard a business organization as a social as well as an economic phenomenon."

The second class of statements includes both descriptions of and inductions from experience. They will range from simple descriptions of concrete events to uniformities among them which have been tested within the limits of our experience by observation and experiment. An example of a second-class statement is: "In every large-scale industrial plant the jobs are socially ordered, some carrying more prestige than others." It should be noted that the test of a statement of the first class is its usefulness and convenience. The test of a statement of the second class is observation and experiment.

To the second class of statements has been applied some deductive reasoning, which leads to the third class of statements. These are generally of the form: "If this be the human situation, what does it imply for management practice?" For example: "If workers have conditioned reflexes, and if these conditioned reflexes involve strong sentiments, what is the implication for wage administration?" "If the environment of the executive is in good part verbal, and if words mean different things to different people in different places in the organization, what is the implication for the problem of communication in a business organization?" Frequently these statements will take the form: "People assume *this* about the motivation and behavior of workers. Observation and experiment show *that* about the motivation and behavior of workers. How come?"

Although the writer has tried to limit himself to these three classes of statements, it would be extraordinary if he were completely successful. On occasion he has probably unconsciously allowed his own sentiments to intrude. Moreover, he has probably allowed the sentiments of his audience to influence him in the direction of saying things in a manner which he hoped would gain their support, challenge their customary ways of thinking, evoke their interest and curiosity. In this attempt he has also probably not been entirely successful. Where statements involving sentiments distasteful to a reader do occur, it is hoped that they can be ignored without detracting from the general point that is being made. In some instances, they can be rephrased so as to coincide with the reader's experience rather than with the writer's sentiments.

CHAPTER II

THE ROAD BACK TO SANITY

AT a recent meeting the researches in personnel at the Hawthorne plant of the Western Electric Company were mentioned by both a management man and a union man. There seemed to be no difference of opinion between the two regarding the importance or relevance of these research findings for effective management-employee relations. This seemed to me interesting because it suggested that the labor situation can be discussed at a level where both sides can roughly agree. The question of what this level is can be answered only after closer examination of these studies.

In the February, 1941, issue of the *Reader's Digest* there appeared a summary statement of these researches by Stuart Chase, under the title, "What Makes the Worker Like to Work?" At the conclusion of his article, Stuart Chase said, "There is an idea here so big that it leaves one gasping." Just what Mr. Chase meant by this statement is not explained, but to find out one can go back to the actual studies and see what was learned from them. In my opinion, the results were very simple and obvious—as Sherlock Holmes used to say to Dr. Watson, "Elementary, my dear Watson." Now this is what may have left Stuart Chase "gasping"—the systematic exploitation of the simple and the obvious which these studies represent.

There seems to be an assumption today that we need a complex set of ideas to handle the complex problems of this complex world in which we live. We assume that a big problem needs a big idea; a complex problem needs a complex idea for its solution. As a result, our thinking tends to become more and more tortuous and muddled. Nowhere is this more true than in matters of human behavior. It seems to me that the road back to sanity — and here is where my title comes in — lies

(1) In having a few simple and clear ideas about the world in which we live.

(2) In complicating our ideas, not in a vacuum, but only in reference to things we can observe, see, feel, hear, and touch. Let us not generalize from verbal definitions; let us know in fact what we are talking about.

(3) In having a very simple method by means of which we can explore our complex world. We need a tool which will allow us to get the data from which our generalizations are to be drawn. We need a simple skill to keep us in touch with what is sometimes referred to as "reality."

(4) In being "tough-minded," i.e. in not letting ourselves be too disappointed because the complex world never quite fulfills our most cherished expectations of it. Let us remember that the concrete phenomena will always elude any set of abstractions that we can make of them.

(5) In knowing very clearly the class of phenomena to which our ideas and methods relate. Now, this is merely a way of saying, "Do not use a saw as a hammer." A saw is a useful tool precisely because it is limited and designed for a certain purpose. Do not criticize the usefulness of a saw because it does not make a good hammer.

Although this last statement is obvious with regard to such things as "saws" and "hammers," it is less well understood in the area of human relations. Too often we try to solve human problems with nonhuman tools and, what is still more extraordinary, in terms of nonhuman data. We take data from which all human meaning has been deleted and then are surprised to find that we reach conclusions which have no human significance.

It is my simple thesis that a human problem requires a human solution. First, we have to learn to recognize a human problem when we see one; and, second, upon recognizing it, we have to learn to deal with it as such and not as if it were something else. Too often at the verbal level we talk glibly about the importance of the human factor; and too seldom at the concrete level of behavior do we recognize a human problem for what it is and deal with it as such. *A human problem to be brought to a human solution requires human data and human tools.* It is my purpose to use the Western Electric researches as an illustration of what I mean by this statement, because, if they deserve the publicity and acclaim which they have received, it is because, in my opinion, they have so conclusively demonstrated this point. In this sense they are the road back to sanity in management-employee relations.

EXPERIMENTS IN ILLUMINATION

The Western Electric researches started about sixteen years ago, in the Hawthorne plant, with a series of experiments on illumination. The purpose was to find out the relation of the quality and quantity of illumination to the efficiency of industrial workers. These studies lasted several years, and I shall not describe them in detail. It will suffice to point out that the results were quite different from what had been expected.

In one experiment the workers were divided into two groups. One group, called the "test group," was to work under different illumination intensities. The other group, called the "control group," was to work under an intensity of illumination as nearly constant as possible. During the first experiment, the test group was submitted to three different intensities of illumination of increasing magnitude, 24, 46, and 70 foot candles. What were the results of this early experiment? Production increased in both rooms — in both the test group and the control group — and the rise in output was roughly of the same magnitude in both cases.

In another experiment, the light under which the test group worked was decreased from 10 to 3 foot candles, while the control group worked, as before, under a constant level of illumination intensity. In this case the output rate in the test group went up instead of down. It also went up in the control group.

In still another experiment, the workers were allowed to believe that the illumination was being increased, although, in fact, no change in intensity was made. The workers commented favorably on the improved lighting condition, but there was no appreciable change in output. At another time, the workers were allowed to believe that the intensity of illumination was being decreased, although again, in fact, no actual change was made. The workers complained somewhat about the poorer lighting, but again there was no appreciable effect on output.

And finally, in another experiment, the intensity of illumination was decreased to .06 of a foot candle, which is the intensity of illumination approximately equivalent to that of ordinary moonlight. Not until this point was reached was there any appreciable decline in the output rate.

What did the experimenters learn? Obviously, as Stuart Chase said, there was something "screwy," but the experimenters were not quite sure who or what was screwy — they themselves, the subjects, or the results. One thing was clear: the results were negative. Nothing of a positive nature had been learned about the relation of illumination to industrial efficiency. If the results were to be taken at their face value, it would appear that there was no relation between illumination and industrial efficiency. However, the investigators were not yet quite willing to draw this conclusion. They realized the difficulty of testing for the effect of a single variable in a situation where there were many uncontrolled variables. It was thought therefore that another experiment should be devised in which other variables affecting the output of workers could be better controlled.

A few of the tough-minded experimenters already were beginning to suspect their basic ideas and assumptions with regard to human motivation. It occurred to them that the trouble was not so much with the results or with the subjects as it was with their notion regarding the way their subjects were supposed to behave — the notion of a simple cause-and-effect, direct relationship between certain physical changes in the workers' environment and the responses of the workers to these changes. Such a notion completely ignored the human meaning of these changes to the people who were subjected to them.

In the illumination experiments, therefore, we have a classic example of trying to deal with a human situation in nonhuman terms. The experimenters had obtained no human data; they had been handling electric-light bulbs and plotting average output curves. Hence their results had no human significance. That is why they seemed screwy. Let me suggest here, however, that the results were not screwy, but the experimenters were — a "screwy" person being by definition one who is not acting in accordance with the customary human values of the situation in which he finds himself.

THE RELAY ASSEMBLY TEST ROOM

Another experiment was framed, in which it was planned to submit a segregated group of workers to different kinds of working conditions. The idea was very simple: A group of five girls were placed in a separate room where their conditions of work could be carefully controlled, where their output could be measured, and where they could be closely observed. It was decided to introduce at specified intervals different changes in working conditions and to see what effect these innovations had on output. Also, records were kept, such as the temperature and humidity of the room, the number of hours each girl slept at night, the kind and amount of food she ate for breakfast, lunch, and dinner. Output was carefully measured, the time it took each girl to assemble a telephone relay of approximately forty parts (roughly a minute) being automatically recorded each time; quality records were kept; each girl had a physical examination at regular intervals. Under these conditions of close observation the girls were studied for a period of five years. Literally tons of material were collected. Probably nowhere in the world has so much material been collected about a small group of workers for such a long period of time.

But what about the results? They can be stated very briefly. When all is said and done, they amount roughly to this: A skillful statistician spent several years trying to relate variations in output with variations in the physical circumstances of these five operators. For example, he correlated the hours that each girl spent in bed the night before with variations in output the following day. Inasmuch as some people said that the effect of being out late one night was not felt the following day but the day after that, he correlated variations in output with the amount of rest the operators had had two nights before. I mention this just to point out the fact that he missed no obvious tricks and that he did a careful job and a thorough one, and it took him many years to do it. The attempt to relate changes in physical circumstances to variations in output resulted in not a single correlation of enough statistical significance to be recognized by any competent statistician as having any meaning.

Now, of course, it would be misleading to say that this negative result was the only conclusion reached. There were positive conclusions, and it did not take the experimenters more than two years to find out that they had missed the boat. After two years of work, certain things happened which made them sit up and take notice. Different experimental conditions of work, in the nature of changes in the number and duration of rest pauses and differences in the length of the working day and week, had been introduced in this Relay Assembly Test Room. For example, the investigators first introduced two five-minute rests, one in the morning and one in the afternoon. Then they increased the length of these rests, and after that they introduced the rests at different times of the day. During one experimental period they served the operators a specially prepared lunch during the rest. In the later periods, they decreased the length of the working day by one-half hour and then by one hour. They gave the operators Saturday morning off for a while. Altogether, thirteen such periods of different working conditions were introduced in the first two years.

During the first year and a half of the experiment, everybody was happy, both the investigators and the operators. The investigators were happy because as conditions of work improved the output rate rose steadily. Here, it appeared, was strong evidence in favor of their preconceived hypothesis that fatigue was the major factor limiting output. The operators were happy because their conditions of work were being improved, they were earning more money, and they were objects of considerable attention from top management. But then one investigator — one of those tough-minded fellows — suggested that they restore the original conditions of work, that is, go back to a full forty-eight-hour week without rests, lunches and what not. This was Period XII. Then the happy state of affairs, when everything was going along as it theoretically should, went sour. Output, instead of taking the expected nose dive, maintained its high level.

Again the investigators were forcibly reminded that human situations are likely to be complex. In any human situation, whenever a simple change is introduced — a rest pause, for example — other changes, unwanted and unanticipated, may also be brought about. What I am saying here is very simple. If one experiments on a stone, the stone does not know it is being experimented upon — all of which makes it simple for people experimenting on stones. But if a human being is being experimented upon, he is likely to know it. Therefore, his attitudes toward the experiment and toward the experimenters become very important factors in determining his responses to the situation.

Now that is what happened in the Relay Assembly Test Room. To the investigators, it was essential that the workers give their full and whole-hearted coöperation to the experiment. They did not want the operators to work harder or easier depending upon their attitude toward the conditions that were imposed. They wanted them to work as they felt, so that they could be sure that the different physical conditions of work were solely responsible for the variations in output. For each of the experimental changes, they wanted subjects whose responses would be uninfluenced by so-called "psychological factors."

In order to bring this about, the investigators did everything in their power to secure the complete coöperation of their subjects, with the result that almost all the practices common to the shop were altered. The operators were consulted about the changes to be made, and, indeed, several plans were abandoned because they met with the disapproval of the girls. They were questioned sympathetically about their reactions to the conditions imposed, and many of these conferences took place in the office of the superintendent. The girls were allowed to talk at work; their "bogey" was eliminated. Their physical health and well-being became matters of great concern. Their opinions, hopes, and fears were eagerly sought. What happened was that in the very process of setting the conditions for the test — a so-called "controlled" experiment — the experimenters had completely altered the social situation of the room. Inadvertently a change had been introduced which was far more important than the planned experimental innovations: the customary supervision in the room had been revolutionized. This accounted for the better attitudes of the girls and their improved rate of work.

THE DEVELOPMENT OF A NEW AND MORE FRUITFUL POINT OF VIEW

After Period XII in the Relay Assembly Test Room, the investigators decided to change their ideas radically. What all their experiments had dramatically and conclusively demonstrated was the importance of employee attitudes and sentiments. It was clear that the responses of workers to what was happening about them were dependent upon the significance these events had for them. In most work situations the meaning of a change is likely to be as important, if not more so, than the change itself. This was the great *éclaircissement,* the new illumination, that came from the research. It was an illumination quite different from what they had expected from the illumination studies. Curiously enough, this discovery is nothing very new or startling. It is something which anyone who has had some concrete experience in handling other people intuitively recognizes and practices. Whether or not a person is going to give his services whole-heartedly to a group depends, in good part, on the way he feels about his job, his fellow workers, and supervisors — the meaning for him of what is happening about him.

However, when the experimenters began to tackle the problem of employee attitudes and the factors determining such attitudes — when they began to tackle the problem of "meaning" — they entered a sort of twilight zone where things are never quite what they seem. Moreover, overnight, as it were, they were robbed of all the tools they had so carefully forged; for all their previous tools were nonhuman tools concerned with the measurement of output, temperature, humidity, etc., and these were no longer useful for the human data that they now wanted to obtain. What the experimenters now wanted to know was how a person felt, what his intimate thinking, reflections, and preoccupations were, and what he liked and disliked about his work environment. In short, what did the whole blooming business — his job, his supervision, his working conditions — mean to him? Now this was human stuff, and there were no tools, or at least the experimenters knew of none, for obtaining and evaluating this kind of material.

Fortunately, there were a few courageous souls among the experimenters. These men were not metaphysicians, psychologists, academicians, professors, intellectuals, or what have you. They were men of common sense and of practical affairs. They were not driven by any great heroic desire to change the world. They were true experimenters, that is, men compelled to follow the implications of their own monkey business. All the evidence of their studies was pointing in one direction. Would they take the jump? They did.

EXPERIMENTS IN INTERVIEWING WORKERS

A few tough-minded experimenters decided to go into the shops and — completely disarmed and denuded of their elaborate logical equipment and in all humility — to see if they could learn how to get the workers to talk about things that were important to them and could learn to understand what the workers were trying to tell them. This was a revolutionary idea in the year 1928, when this interviewing program started — the idea of getting a worker to talk to you and to listen sympathetically, but intelligently, to what he had to say. In that year a new era of personnel relations began. It was the first real attempt to get human data and to forge human tools to get them. In that year a novel idea was born; dimly the experimenters perceived a new method of human control. In that year the Rubicon was crossed from which there could be no return to the "good old days." Not that the experimenters ever wanted to return, because they now entered a world so exciting, so intriguing, and so full of promise that it made the "good old days" seem like the prattle and play of children.

When these experimenters decided to enter the world of "meaning," with very few tools, but with a strong sense of curiosity and a willingness to learn, they had many interesting adventures. It would be too long a story to tell all of them, or even a small part of them. They made plenty of mistakes, but they were not afraid to learn.

At first, they found it difficult to learn to give full and complete attention to what a person had to say without interrupting him before he was through. They found it difficult to learn not to give advice, not to make or imply moral judgments about the speaker, not to argue, not to be too clever, not to dominate the conversation, not to ask leading questions. They found it difficult to get the person to talk about matters which were important to him and not to the interviewer. But, most important of all, they found it difficult to learn that perhaps the thing most significant to a person was not something in his immediate work situation.

Gradually, however, they learned these things. They discovered that sooner or later a person tends to talk about what is uppermost in his mind to a sympathetic and skillful listener, and they became more proficient in interpreting what a person is saying or trying to say. Of course they protected the confidences given to them and made absolutely sure that nothing an employee said could ever be used against him. Slowly they began to forge a simple human tool — imperfect, to be sure — to get the kind of data they wanted. They called this method "interviewing." I would hesitate to say the number of man-hours of labor which went into the forging of this tool. There followed from studies made through its use a gradually changing conception of the worker and his behavior.

A NEW WAY OF VIEWING EMPLOYEE SATISFACTION AND DISSATISFACTION

When the experimenters started to study employee likes and dislikes, they assumed, at first, that they would find a simple and logical relation between a person's likes or dislikes and certain items and events in his immediate work situation. They expected to find a simple connection, for example, between a person's complaint and the object about which he was complaining. Hence, the solution would be easy: correct the object of the complaint, if possible, and presto! the complaint would disappear. Unfortunately, however, the world of human behavior is not so simple as this conception of it; and it took the investigators several arduous and painful years to find this out. I will mention only a few interesting experiences they had.

Several times they changed the objects of the complaint only to find that the attitudes of the complainants remained unchanged. In these cases, correcting the object of the complaint did not remedy the complaint or the attitude of the person expressing it. A certain complaint might disappear, to be sure, only to have another one arise. Here the investigators were running into so-called "chronic kickers," people whose dissatisfactions were more deeply rooted in factors relating to their personal histories. For such people the simple remedy of changing the object of the complaint was not enough.

Several times they did absolutely nothing about the object of the complaint, but after the interview, curiously enough, the complaint disappeared. A typical example of this was that of a woman who complained at great length and with considerable feeling about the poor food being served in the company restaurant. When, a few days later, she chanced to meet the interviewer, she commented with great enthusiasm upon the improved food and thanked the interviewer for communicating her grievance to management and for securing such prompt action. Here no change had been made in the thing criticized; yet the employee felt that something had been done.

Many times they found that people did not really want anything done about the things of which they were complaining. What they did want was an opportunity to talk about their troubles to a sympathetic listener. It was astonishing to find the number of instances in which workers complained about things which had happened many, many years ago, but which they described as vividly as if they had happened just a day before.

Here again, something was "screwy," but this time the experimenters realized that it was their assumptions which were screwy. They were assuming that the meanings which people assign to their experience are essentially logical. They were carrying in their heads the notion of the "economic man," a man primarily motivated by economic interest, whose logical capacities were being used in the service of this self-interest.

Gradually and painfully in the light of the evidence, which was overwhelming, the experimenters had been forced to abandon this conception of the worker and his behavior. Only with a new working hypothesis could they make sense of the data they had collected. The conception of the worker which they developed is actually nothing very new or startling; it is one which any effective administrator intuitively recognizes and practices in handling human beings.

First, they found that the behavior of workers could not be understood apart from their feelings or sentiments. I shall use the word "sentiment" hereafter to refer not only to such things as feelings and emotions, but also to a much wider range of phenomena which may not be expressed in violent feelings or emotions—phenomena that are referred to by such words as "loyalty," "integrity," "solidarity."

Secondly, they found that sentiments are easily disguised, and hence are difficult to recognize and to study. Manifestations of sentiment take a number of different forms. Feelings of personal integrity, for example, can be expressed by a handshake; they can also be expressed, when violated, by a sitdown strike. Moreover, people like to rationalize their sentiments and to objectify them. We are not so likely to say "I feel bad," as to say "The world is bad." In other words, we like to endow the world with those attributes and qualities which will justify and account for the feelings and sentiments we have toward it; we tend to project our sentiments on the outside world.

Thirdly, they found that manifestations of sentiment could not be understood as things in and by themselves, but only in terms of the total situation of the person. To comprehend why a person felt the way he did, a wider range of phenomena had to be explored. The following three diagrams illustrate roughly the development of this point of view.

It will be remembered that at first the investigators assumed a simple and direct relation between certain physical changes in the worker's environment and his responses to them. This simple state of mind is illustrated in diagram I. But all the evidence of the early experiments showed that the responses of employees to changes in their immediate working environment can be understood only in terms of their attitudes — the "meaning" these changes have for them. This point of view is represented in diagram II. However, the "meaning" which these changes have for the worker is not strictly and primarily logical, for they are fraught with human feelings and values. The "meaning," therefore, which any individual worker assigns to a particular change depends upon (1) his social "conditioning," or what sentiments (values, hopes, fears, expectations, etc.) he is bringing to the work situation because of his previous family and group associations, and hence the relation of the change to these sentiments; and (2) the kind of human satisfactions he is deriving from his social participation with other workers and supervisors in the immediate work group of which he is a member, and hence the effect of the change on his customary interpersonal relations. This way of

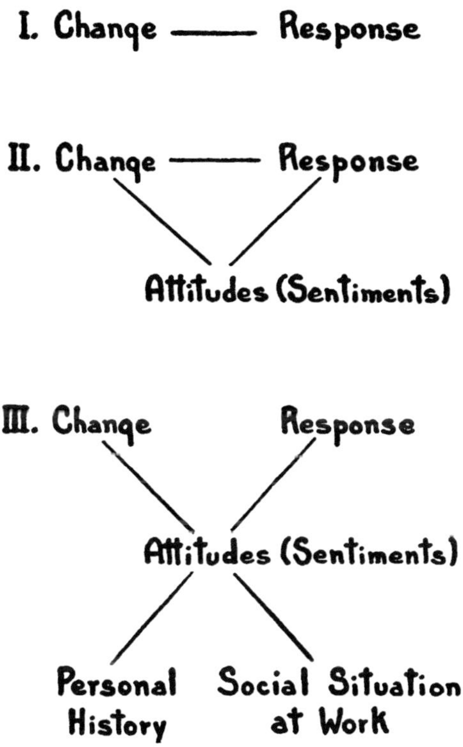

regarding the responses of workers (both verbal and overt) is represented in diagram III. It says briefly: Sentiments do not appear in a vacuum; they do not come out of the blue; they appear in a social context. They have to be considered in terms of that context, and apart from it they are likely to be misunderstood.

One further point should be made about that aspect of the

worker's environment designated "Social Situation at Work" in diagram III. What is meant is that the worker is not an isolated, atomic individual; he is a member of a group, or of groups. Within each of these groups the individuals have feelings and sentiments toward each other, which bind them together in collaborative effort. Moreover, these collective sentiments can, and do, become attached to every item and object in the industrial environment — even to output. Material goods, output, wages, hours of work, and so on, cannot be treated as things in themselves. Instead, they must be interpreted as carriers of social value.

OUTPUT AS A FORM OF SOCIAL BEHAVIOR

That output is a form of social behavior was well illustrated in a study made by the Hawthorne experimenters, called the Bank Wiring Observation Room. This room contained fourteen workmen representing three occupational groups — wiremen, soldermen, and inspectors. These men were on group piecework, where the more they turned out the more they earned. In such a situation one might have expected that they would have been interested in maintaining total output and that the faster workers would have put pressure on the slower workers to improve their efficiency. But this was not the case. Operating within this group were four basic sentiments, which can be expressed briefly as follows: (1) You should not turn out too much work; if you do, you are a "rate buster." (2) You should not turn out too little work; if you do, you are a "chiseler." (3) You should not say anything to a supervisor which would react to the detriment of one of your associates; if you do, you are a "squealer." (4) You should not be too officious; that is, if you are an inspector you should not act like one.

To be an accepted member of the group a man had to act in accordance with these social standards. One man in this group exceeded the group standard of what constituted a fair day's work. Social pressure was put on him to conform, but without avail, since he enjoyed doing things the others disliked. The best-liked person in the group was the one who kept his output exactly where the group agreed it should be.

Inasmuch as the operators were agreed as to what constituted a day's work, one might have expected rate of output to be about the same for each member of the group. This was by no means the case; there were marked differences. At first the experimenters thought that the differences in individual performance were related to differences in ability, so they compared each worker's relative rank in output with his relative rank in intelligence and dexterity as measured by certain tests. The results were interesting: the lowest producer in the room ranked first in intelligence and third in dexterity; the highest producer in the room was seventh in dexterity and lowest in intelligence. Here surely was a situation in which the native capacities of the men were not finding expression. From the viewpoint of logical, economic behavior, this room did not make sense. Only in terms of powerful sentiments could these individual differences in output level be explained. Each worker's level of output reflected his position in the informal organization of the group.

WHAT MAKES THE WORKER NOT WANT TO COÖPERATE

As a result of the Bank Wiring Observation Room, the Hawthorne researchers became more and more interested in the informal employee groups which tend to form within the formal organization of the company, and which are not likely to be represented in the organization chart. They became interested in the beliefs and creeds which have the effect of making each individual feel an integral part of the group and which make the group appear as a single unit, in the social codes and norms of behavior by means of which employees automatically work together in a group without any conscious choice as to whether they will or will not coöperate. They studied the important social functions these groups perform for their members, the histories of these informal work groups, how they spontaneously appear, how they tend to perpetuate themselves, multiply, and disappear, how they are in constant jeopardy from technical change, and hence how they tend to resist innovation. In particular, they became interested in those groups whose norms and codes of behavior are at variance with the technical and economic objectives of the company as a whole. They examined the social conditions under which it is more likely for the employee group to separate itself out in opposition to the remainder of the groups which make up the total organization. In such phenomena they felt that they had at last arrived at the heart of the problem of effective collaboration. They obtained a new enlightenment of the present industrial scene; from this point of view, many perplexing problems became more intelligible.

Some people claim, for example, that the size of the pay envelope is the major demand which the employee is making of his job. All the worker wants is to be told what to do and to get paid for doing it. If we look at him and his job in terms of sentiments, this is far from being as generally true as we would like to believe. Most of us want the satisfaction that comes from being accepted and recognized as people of worth by our friends and work associates. Money is only a small part of this social recognition. The way we are greeted by our boss, being asked to help a newcomer, being asked to keep an eye on a difficult operation, being given a job requiring special skill — all of these are acts of social recognition. They tell us how we stand in our work group. We all want tangible evidence of our social importance. We want to have a skill that is socially recognized as useful. We want the feeling of security that comes not so much from the amount of money we have in the bank as from being an accepted member of a group. A man whose job is without social function is like a man without a country; the activity to which he has to give the major portion of his life is robbed of all human meaning and significance.

If this is true — and all the evidence of the Western Electric researches points in this direction — have we not a clue as to the possible basis for labor unrest and disputes? Granted that these disputes are often stated in terms of wages, hours of work, and physical conditions of work, is it not possible that these demands are disguising, or in part are the symptomatic expression of, much more deeply rooted human situations which we have not as yet learned to recognize, to understand, or to control? It has been said there is an irresistible urge on the part of workers to tell the boss off, to tell the boss to go to hell. For some workers this generalization may hold, and I have no reason to believe it does not. But, in those situations where it does, it is telling us something very important about these particular workers and their work situations. Workers who want to tell their boss to go to hell sound to me like people whose feelings of personal integrity have been seriously injured. What in their work situations has shattered their feelings of personal integrity? Until we understand better the answer to this question, we cannot handle effectively people who manifest such sentiments. Without such understanding we are dealing only with words and not with human situations — as I fear our overlogicized machinery for handling employee grievances sometimes does.

The matters of importance to workers which the Hawthorne researches disclosed are not settled primarily by negotiating contracts. If industry today is filled with people living in a social void and without social function, a labor contract can do little to make coöperation possible. If, on the other hand, the workers are an integral part of the social situations in which they work, a legal contract is not of the first importance. Too many of us are more interested in getting our words legally straight than in getting our situations humanly straight.

In summary, therefore, the Western Electric researches seem to me like a beginning on the road back to sanity in employee relations because (1) they offer a fruitful working hypothesis, a few simple and relatively clear ideas for the study and understanding of human situations in business; (2) they offer a simple method by means of which we can explore and deal with the complex human problems in a business organization — this method is a human method: it deals with things which are important to people; and (3) they throw a new light on the precondition for effective collaboration. Too often we think of collaboration as something which can be logically or legally contrived. The Western Electric studies indicate that it is far more a matter of sentiment than a matter of logic. Workers are not isolated, unrelated individuals; they are social animals and should be treated as such.

This statement — the worker is a social animal and should be treated as such — is simple, but the systematic and consistent practice of this point of view is not. If it were systematically practiced, it would revolutionize present-day personnel work. Our technological development in the past hundred years has been tremendous. Our methods of handling people are still archaic. If this civilization is to survive, we must obtain a new understanding of human motivation and behavior in business organizations — an understanding which can be simply but effectively practiced. The Western Electric researches contribute a first step in this direction.

CHAPTER III

UNDERSTANDING: A PREREQUISITE OF LEADERSHIP

INDUSTRY is a social as well as an economic phenomenon. An industrial concern is not only an organization for the promotion of economic purposes; it is also a human organization in which the hopes and aspirations of individuals are trying to find expression. In these terms the leader of an industrial enterprise has two functions to fulfill, an economic function and a social function. First, he has to manufacture and distribute a product at a profit. Second, he has to keep individuals and groups of individuals working effectively together. A great deal of attention has been given to the first function. Scientific controls have been introduced to further the economic purposes of a concern and of the individuals within it. Much of this advance has gone on in the name of efficiency or rationalization. Nothing comparable to this advance has gone on in the personal relations between employer and employee. Whatever slight advance there may have been is completely overshadowed by the new and powerful technology of modern industry. One important reason for this difference is not difficult to find. Effective relations between employer and employee largely reside in skills that are personal, empirical, and intuitive — skills which the individual utilizing them cannot make very explicit. Unlike the skills developed in the technological area, they are difficult to communicate. To them science has been little applied.

Numberless examples could be cited to show that these two skills, technical skill and skill in dealing with human relations, do not necessarily go hand in hand in the same individual.

There are some men highly intelligent and logical within their areas of specialty who at the same time are bunglers in the art of human relations. Likewise, there are some men highly skilled in the handling of people for whose logical capacities one can have little respect. That high logical skill and skill in handling people do not necessarily go together suggests that they are concerned with different factors. It suggests that, in handling human relations, logic alone will not avail.

In matters pertaining to human collaboration, sentiments and the interaction of the sentiments are important phenomena. Any development of communicable skills in the area of human relations, comparable to those in the technical area, therefore presupposes an understanding of the nature of sentiments.

SOME PROPERTIES OF SENTIMENTS

A simple way of explaining what I mean by sentiments is to differentiate them from another class of phenomena with which they are often confused, namely, facts. Facts have two essential properties: they are conclusions about matters of observation, and they involve terms for which there exist certain operations that can be agreed upon as defining them.

Should I say, "The temperature of this room is 72° F.," everyone would agree that that statement is either fact or error. Should anyone wish to challenge my statement, we should all agree as to the method by means of which the statement could be tested, verified, or corroborated, and we should all abide by the decision of this independent judge, the thermometer. But now let me make another judgment. This time I say, "The room is too hot." Some may agree, and others may disagree with this judgment. Let me assume that someone who disagrees with me wishes to convince me that my statement is incorrect. Let me assume that he says, "But, my dear fellow, the temperature in this room is 68°," and he shows me a thermometer to convince me. I look at the thermometer, agree with him that it registers 68° F. But does that convince me? No. I disagree with his definition of "too hot" as being any thermometer reading above 68° F. I may come back at him and say, "Look here, old man, I'm giving a talk in this room and for the speaker a room at 68° is too hot." At this point he is likely to say, "Don't be silly," meaning that he disagrees with my definition of "too hot." Indirectly he is telling me that I can't define a room as "too hot" in this way. Now what do I do? At this point I'm likely to retort, "Says who?" meaning who is he to tell me how I am going to define the term "too hot." In short, all his attempts to convince me end in a verbal argument because any attempts at verification involve an arbitrary definition of what is "too hot,"[1] upon which we cannot agree.

The first judgment I made was capable of verification. It was either fact or error. The second judgment I made was an expression of sentiment. *It was neither fact nor error.* Strictly speaking, expressions of sentiment are neither true nor false. They refer to the personal and social life of the person who expresses them. Apart from such a context they are meaningless. They cannot be assessed apart from the individual who makes them. Or, to put it another way, sentiments are biologically, psychologically, or socially determined. They vary with time, place, sex, age, nationality, personality, social status, and temperament, to mention some of the many factors. To go back to the previous example: a room at 68° may be called "comfortable" by an Englishman, "cold" by an American, "hot" by a man who is doing heavy muscular work, "chilly" by a man sitting at a desk, "suffocating" by Byrd at Little America, and "too hot" by a nervous man unexpectedly called upon to make a speech.

[1] For a more complete discussion of the difference between fact and sentiment, see L. J. Henderson, "Science, Logic and Human Intercourse," *Harvard Business Review*, vol. XII, no. 3, April, 1934, pp. 317–327.

Sentiments refer not only to "hots" and "colds" but also to a vast range of feelings, emotions, and attitudes, some of which are normal, some of which are pathological. They include behavior patterns which may appear ugly — fear, anger, jealousy, and envy, for instance — and behavior patterns regarded as beautiful, such as loyalty, courage, devotion, honesty, truth, and goodness. They include those things within people which are appealed to by such statements as the following: "The Constitution should be preserved"; "There can be only one capital, Washington or Berlin"; and "Woman's place is in the home."

This statement that the human being has sentiments, and that therefore it is very important for the leader to be aware of this fact, does not imply that the human being is "sentimental" according to popular meaning, that the human being is irrational, or that sentiments should be eliminated from human beings. What it does imply is that the human being is a social animal and that a social animal is not merely — in fact, is very seldom — motivated by matters pertaining strictly to fact or logic. However, to conclude from this statement that therefore all human responses not strictly logical are illogical or irrational is a false distinction. Most human behavior is neither logical nor irrational; it is nonlogical, that is to say, it is motivated by sentiment. To eliminate such nonlogical conduct would be to destroy all values and significances, everything which for most of us makes life worth living.

The distinctions between logical, nonlogical, and irrational behavior can be explained by the following example: When I put on my hat in order to protect my head from the heat rays of the sun, I am behaving logically. When I take off my hat upon entering a church, I am behaving nonlogically. Likewise, if I put my hat on when entering a synagogue, I am behaving nonlogically. If for no good reason I throw my new hat on the ground and stamp on it, I am behaving irrationally. Let us assume now, however, that I am a college undergraduate and that it is the code of this group not to wear new-looking hats; then stamping on my hat in order to destroy its new appearance becomes nonlogical. It will be noticed that logical behavior presupposes an objective connection among things that are unaffected by my particular beliefs. Nonlogical behavior, such as taking my hat off to a woman, is action in accordance with the sentiments of correct social behavior in the group to which I belong. Such behavior integrates me to that group. Irrational behavior, on the other hand, although motivated by sentiments, is personal and peculiar to me. Such behavior estranges me from, rather than binds me to, human association.

This consideration brings up another interesting property of sentiments: they cannot be modified by logic alone. When my friend brought me a thermometer registering 68° in order to convince me that my statement was false, he, of course, was under a misapprehension. He thought I was making a statement of fact. Actually, I was expressing my state of mind; I was expressing a sentiment. But my friend was not to blame for his confusion. I didn't express my sentiment as sentiment. I did not say, "I feel hot." I said, "This room is hot." I did try to disguise my sentiment as a statement of fact. Now that is another peculiar property of sentiments. They are frequently disguised as fact or logic. Indeed, two of the most important and time-consuming pastimes of the human mind are to rationalize sentiments and to try to modify sentiments by logic.

Now in this last point there may be a clue to the reason why some individuals who are particularly adept in handling matters of fact and logic fall short when it comes to handling human relations. They are constantly confusing fact with sentiment. They are treating expressions of sentiment as if they were statements of fact. When such a man comes home at night and his wife says, "Man's work is from sun to sun; but woman's work is never done," he immediately gets annoyed with her for her disregard of certain elementary facts about the work of men and the broader responsibilities of men.

When an employee, Bill, comes to this same man's office and says, "My piece rates are too low," this kind of employer immediately goes into a long explanation to the effect that the rates have been set in a most scientific manner on the basis of time and motion studies and that, moreover, these rates are in accordance with rates paid by other concerns in the same territory for comparable work. In other words, he defines to Bill what constitutes a "fair rate," just as my friend tried to define to me what was meant by "too hot." Now it may be that Bill will be interested in this logical definition. The chances are, however, that he will not. He may be trying to tell his employer that his wife is in the hospital, his children are sick, doctors' bills are rapidly accumulating, and he cannot pay them. It may be that in Bill's company there is a fund to take care of such cases, a fund which Bill does not know of but his employer does. However, Bill has no chance to tell his story. He leaves the office disgruntled. Instead of getting human understanding, he gets a logical definition which in all probability only succeeds in increasing his conviction that his piece rates are too low and that he is being treated unfairly.

Sentiments have another interesting property. They are such an intimate part of our mental equipment that often we cannot make them explicit. They act in our thinking as a system of absolute truths. For this reason they enter into the determination of our everyday judgments and thoughts. They constitute our ultimate values and significances in terms of which we assess our everyday world.

Probably the most interesting characteristic of certain sentiments is their tendency to build themselves up into systems, patterns, or configurations. These systems of sentiments also have certain properties. They tend to persist and to resist change. For the industrial leader, there is nothing more important than an understanding of the systems of sentiments which bind individuals together into social groups.[2]

INDUSTRY AS A SYSTEM OF SENTIMENTS

Let us now conceive of an industrial establishment as a system or pattern of sentiments. This way of looking at things will help us to see how every item and event in the industrial environment becomes an object of a system of sentiments. According to this way of looking at things, material goods, physical events, wages, hours of work, and so on, cannot be treated as things in themselves. Instead, they have to be interpreted as carriers of social value.

A cursory examination of any large-scale industrial establishment will reveal that the jobs within it are socially ordered. Some of them carry more prestige and social significance than others. This ordering of significance, it will be found, is reflected in a number of different ways: in methods of payment, in hours of work, and in working conditions. Wages, for example, vary with occupations, and these wage differentials frequently serve to reinforce occupational stratification. Much evidence could be cited to show that the worker is quite as much concerned with these differentials — that is, the relation of his wages to the wages of the other workmen — as with the absolute amount of his wages. In short, the job and all those factors connected with it serve to define the position of the person performing that job in the social organization of the company of which he is a member. That jobs are socially ordered is a fact of the greatest importance. For it will be seen that, in so far as this holds true, any change in the job is likely to alter the existing routine relations between the person whose

[2] See T. N. Whitehead, "Leadership within Industrial Organizations," *Harvard Business Review*, vol. xiv, no. 2, Winter, 1936, pp. 161–171. In this article Mr. Whitehead makes four important generalizations about this group of sentiments.

job it is and other people within the plant. But changes in the social significance of work are not confined to changes in the job alone. The physical task may remain the same, but its social significance may be altered by changes in working conditions. When it is perceived that many such conditions are symbolic of the status of the job, it is easy to understand why this is so. If the only visible difference in two levels of supervision is the size or arrangement of the desk, the color of the carpet, or the kind of calendar pad each supervisor has, that difference, as anyone who has lived in such situations knows, assumes considerable significance, not only to the executives but to the people reporting to them.

The following incident illustrates how important small things may become in a situation permeated with social value: The personnel of a certain department was moved from one building to another. In the new location, because of lack of space, it was found necessary to seat four people across the aisle from the remainder of the group. It happened that there were three women in the department who were to be transferred to other work. These three were given desks across the aisle so that their going would not necessitate a rearrangement of desks. The fourth person, a man, was also given a desk there, simply because there was no other place for him to sit. In choosing the fourth person, the supervisor was undoubtedly influenced by the fact that he was older than the rest of the group and was well acquainted with the three women. But, beyond that, nothing was implied by the fact that he was chosen. Now see how he interpreted this change. He felt that his supervisor regarded him as one of the women. The women were being transferred to other types of work; consequently he too would be transferred before long. Two of the women were being transferred to jobs in the shop. He, himself, might be transferred to the shop; and there was nothing he dreaded more. Having dwelt on speculations like this for a while, the employee recalled with alarm that his name had been omitted from the current issue of the house telephone directory. This omission had been quite accidental. The house telephone directory, however, constituted in this concern a sort of social register. Names of shop people below the rank of assistant foreman were not printed unless they were employed in some special capacity requiring contacts with other organizations. With the exception of typists and certain clerical groups, the names of all office people were listed. The fact that his name had been omitted now took on new significance. It tended to reinforce his growing conviction that he was about to be transferred to an unimportant shop position. He became so preoccupied with the problem that he could not work. He was completely demoralized.

Now from a rational point of view it may seem silly for this employee to have drawn so many erroneous conclusions; but, like most social beings, he was responding to certain social signals. In this case, however, the signals got twisted.

FIVE SOCIAL GROUPS IN INDUSTRY

Looking at an industrial plant from the point of view of sentiments reveals another important fact. It shows that no simple twofold classification of the personnel can be made — into employers and employees, for instance, or management and workers, or supervisors and employees. In any plant of moderate size such an inspection will reveal at least five groups whose interrelations need to be considered:

(1) A group of people in whom responsibility for the concern as a whole is vested, which is generally called management.

(2) A group of supervisors through whom in part management exercises control. This group is not so much concerned with general administrative problems as with getting a job done and carrying out the orders of the managerial group.

(3) A group of technical specialists through whom in part management also exercises control, which includes the highly trained engineer, the efficiency expert, the cost accountant, and the rate setter.

(4) A group of office workers and clerical assistants.

(5) A group of shop, bench, and machine workers.

A study of the interrelations among these five groups reveals some interesting results. It shows how, unwittingly, the attempt to rationalize industry at the expense of social sentiments may produce a constraint type of morality. Consider first the relation between the technologist and the worker.

The Relation between the Technologist and the Worker

Perhaps the chief characteristic of the technologist group of persons is that they are experimentally minded. They think in terms of the logic of efficiency, and they scrutinize everything that comes within their scope in these terms. This group is constantly striving to make improvements in machines, mechanical processes, and products. Sometimes they devise ingenious ways of bringing the worker's actions in line with the logic of efficiency. If the assumptions on which such plans are based be granted, they are perfectly sound. Certainly the technologist has no intention of foisting an arbitrary set of rules upon the worker. In fact, most of his plans are designed to help the worker. Carefully thought out wage plans are intended to reimburse the worker with a wage proportional to his efforts. The simplification of his job, whether through a change in process, division of labor, or elimination of random movements, is supposed to make his work easier and less fatiguing. If fatigue is eliminated, the worker, theoretically, can produce more and can thereby earn more money.

Now it happens frequently that these logical plans to promote efficiency and collaboration do not work out as intended. From the point of view of sentiments, they involve consequences which sometimes defeat the logical purposes of the plan as conceived. Let me point out some of these possible nonlogical consequences. When skill is divorced from the job at the work level and put in the hands of a group of technologists, a situation is created whereby the worker is put in a position of having to accommodate himself continually to changes which he does not initiate. And not only is he asked to accommodate himself to changes which he does not initiate, but also many of these changes deprive him of those very things which give meaning and significance to his work. In the language of the sentiments, it is as if the worker were told that his own individual skills, his acquired routines of work, his cultural traditions of craftsmanship, his personal interrelations, had absolutely no value. Now, such nonlogical consequences have devastating effects on the individual. They make him feel insecure, frustrated, or exasperated.

The Relation between the Supervisor and the Worker

Unlike the technologist, the supervisor is related to the worker in a direct, personal, face-to-face way. Moreover, the supervisor has disciplinary authority over the worker. To say that one person has disciplinary authority over another is to say that the superior is under the obligation of seeing that his subordinate's conduct is in accord with certain prescribed norms. The father-son relationship, for example, contains this element of disciplinary authority. But let us see how it differs from the supervisor-employee relationship in terms of the norms of conduct with reference to which discipline is exercised. In the case of the father-son relationship these norms are set by society at large. The father disciplines the son into socially controlled and socially approved modes of behavior, and he is aided in that process by numerous social institutions, such as the church and school. In the case of the supervisor-employee relationship, no similar social codes exist. The criterion in terms of which the supervisor must exercise discipline is not the convention of ordinary social living, but the logic of efficiency. He has to be constantly insisting that the worker's behavior correspond to what the logic of efficiency represents it to be. But what does the logic of efficiency represent the worker's behavior to be? It assumes that the worker is a logical being, primarily motivated by economic interest, who will see the various technical systems set up for his economic interests as the creators of these systems see them; namely, as logical, coherent schemes which the worker can use, and should use, to his own advantage. However, some matters do not work out as the strict logic of the situation dictates. In human situations things do not mean to individuals what they are logically intended to mean. They are or they mean what human sentiments interpret them to be or to mean. And so here we have the paradox: The very schemes management devises to promote collaboration may become the very factors which prevent effective collaboration. What in the language of efficiency is intended as a source of help may become, when translated into the language of sentiments, a source of constraint.

The supervisor is in a difficult situation. More than any other person, he knows that it is impossible to uphold strictly the logic of efficiency without sometimes demoralizing his group. Many rules which he is supposed to enforce and which, in terms of technical efficiency, should promote efficiency and thereby redound to the worker's advantage, become in terms of the worker's sentiments petty annoyances which deprive his work of social significance. So the supervisor is put in a position of having to give lip service to a point of view which it would be suicidal to practice. He has to talk in one way and behave in another.

In one department, for example, where three occupational groups were working together (wiremen, soldermen, and inspectors) there was an unwritten rule to the effect that not more than two wiremen should help each other in wiring the same equipment. This rule received its sanction from the logic of efficiency, which said that the wiremen could turn out more work by working only on the equipments to which they were assigned. There would be less opportunity for talking, less likelihood of their getting in one another's way, and less likelihood of their delaying the soldermen. To the wiremen, however, this was just another arbitrary rule. Many of them preferred to work together occasionally. It was one of the ways in which they expressed their social solidarity. The supervisor recognized this situation. Moreover, he knew that working together did not necessitate slowing down. In fact, the evidence showed that when the wiremen were refused the privilege of helping one another, they became more inefficient. So occasionally he allowed this type of behavior to continue. By so doing, however, he was running counter to the logic of efficiency, the logic he was under obligation to uphold.

It can be seen that one of the chief sources of constraint in a working group can be a logic of efficiency which does not take into account the worker's sentiments. Any activity not strictly in accordance with the logic of efficiency (and sometimes this means most forms of social behavior) becomes wrong and can only be indulged in surreptitiously. Social activity is driven into the ground, where it forms at a lower level in opposition to the technical organization.

CONCERNING APPLICABILITY

The time has come to restate the question. We started with two assertions: first, that one of the chief functions of an industrial leader is to secure collaboration, and, second, that in matters pertaining to collaboration the sentiments and their interactions are very important. On the ground, therefore, that it is wise to know something about the nature of the phenomenon to be controlled, we looked at the properties of sentiments.

We noticed their stubborn, persistent character in their resistance to rapid change and to modification by logic. We observed their ubiquitous nature. With these characteristics in mind, we examined the industrial environment. We noticed how sentiments are being reflected in the worker's job and in his surrounding conditions. We noticed that even in simple matters, such as the moving of desks and chairs, sentiments are also likely to be manipulated. We saw how the logic of efficiency may appear to the worker as something quite different from what it is intended to be. In short, we elaborated a way of looking at things from the point of view of the sentiments. We erected a more explicit framework for ideas already intuitively derived. But now the question can be raised: Granted that this is a useful way of looking at things, how can it be applied? What are the methods of application?

The application of this point of view to practice is something which some people are doing intuitively all the time. Its skillful application has gone under a number of different names: good breeding, manners, tact, diplomacy, courtesy, personality, charm, wisdom, and understanding. However, there is a method which applies this point of view to practice more explicitly and systematically.

THE INTERVIEWING METHOD

This method is called interviewing. It is a method of assessing a person's attitudes and the factors determining them. Whenever one undergoes this experience of sitting down and patiently listening to an individual, not with the purpose of making any moral judgments, but with the purpose of trying to understand why he feels and acts as he does, a new outlook is likely to develop. One discerns the beginnings of a new method of human control.

During the period from 1928 to 1930 members of the industrial relations staff of the Hawthorne plant of the Western

Electric Company interviewed some 20,000 employees. In the beginning they hoped to get "facts" in the strict sense. From these data they hoped to improve working conditions and company policy. But what they did get from the interviews was an inextricable mixture of fact and sentiment. This outpouring of human sentiments could not be used in the simple fashion originally conceived. However, it is to the credit of management that they did not throw this material into the rubbish heap. They began to see that sentiments, when properly understood and interpreted, constituted social data of the greatest importance.

Probably one of the most interesting developments of this interviewing program was the experience which the interviewers themselves received and in turn communicated to supervisors. When some of the more enterprising of the interviewers realized the nature of the material they were eliciting from employees, they began to devise rules and techniques for ferreting out and trying to understand the employees' sentiments. Curiously enough, the very rules they devised to improve their interviewing technique, they found were easily translatable into simple rules for the supervisor in handling his personal relations. These rules apply to the first-line supervisor, as well as to the higher executive, in his relation to individuals with whom he has face-to-face contacts.[3]

The first rule is that the supervisor should listen patiently to what his subordinate has to say before making any comment himself. Probably the quickest way to stop a person from sufficiently expressing himself is to interrupt. Of course, it follows that, besides actively listening and not interrupting, the supervisor should try to understand what his subordinate is

[3] Some of these rules have already been reported in a preliminary statement of some of the Western Electric Company researches. See Elton Mayo, *The Human Problems of an Industrial Civilization* (New York: Macmillan, 1933), pp. 77–121.

saying. Moreover, he should show his interest in what is being said.

The second rule is that the supervisor should refrain from hasty disapprobation of his subordinate's conduct. It is not his business, in the first instance at least, to give advice or moral admonition. If the employee says, "This is a hell of a company to work for," the attitude of the supervisor should not be, "Tut, tut, my good man, you are not displaying the proper spirit." Instead, he should try to get the employee to express himself more fully by asking why he feels as he does. In many instances employees by themselves are not able to state precisely the particular source of their dissatisfaction, but if they are encouraged to talk freely the effect is not merely emotional relief but also the revelation to the critical listener (and sometimes even to the speaker himself) of the locus of the complaint.

The third rule is that the supervisor should not argue with his subordinate. It is futile to try to change sentiments by logic. The best way for the supervisor to avoid arguments is to see that the employee's sentiments do not act on his own. It will be remembered that when Bill told his employer that his piece rates were too low he acted upon his employer's sentiments. The employer felt that he had to defend his wage rates.

The fourth rule is that the supervisor should not pay exclusive attention to the manifest content of the conversation. The interviewers had discovered that there is a tendency to rationalize sentiments and that in ordinary social intercourse the participants are likely to become more interested in the truth of the rationalizations than in the sentiments that are being expressed. Bill's employer, it will be remembered, paid attention only to the manifest content of Bill's complaint, with the result that he failed to learn anything about Bill's personal situation.

The fifth rule is that the supervisor should listen not only to what a person wants to say but also to what he does not want to say or cannot say without assistance. A person has difficulty in talking about matters which are associated with unpleasant and painful experiences, and many sentiments tend to remain so much in the background of a person's thinking that he is unaware of them. It is important to listen for what a person regards as so obvious and so common that it never occurs to him to doubt or question it. These implicit assumptions are of the greatest importance in assessing a person's values and significances. How often one discerns when listening to people the following assumptions: that everything that is not perfectly safe is dangerous (the common assumption of the hypochondriac); that everything that is not perfectly clean is dirty (the fussy housekeeper); that everything that is not perfectly good is bad (the Puritan); that everything that is not perfectly efficient is inefficient (some efficiency engineers). These are all false distinctions and oversimplifications.[4]

A NEW CONCEPTION OF COLLABORATION AND LEADERSHIP

In short, then, as a result of interviewing experience at Hawthorne, a new conception of leadership was developed. This conception began to percolate to the higher ranks of supervision and to the higher executives of the company. They found that one of their functions as supervisors and managers was to listen to, and become better acquainted with, the sentiments of their employees and with the nature of that social structure, or system of sentiments, called "the company." They began to see that each industrial concern had a social structure, that this social structure was related to the wider social structure of the community. They began to see that it was very important for them to understand their own social

[4] For an interesting discussion of these rules of interviewing as applied to fields other than industry, see L. J. Henderson, "Physician and Patient as a Social System," *The New England Journal of Medicine*, vol. 212, no. 18, May, 1935, pp. 819–823.

structure, for this structure defined the limits and degree of collaboration. When they listened to the complaints of their employees, they realized they were listening to the creakings and groanings of their own social structure. When they saw the newly arrived young college man making an ass of himself, annoyed at the red tape which seemed to block his movements at every turn, they began to realize they were watching the painful adaptations of a logically tutored individual to a complicated social structure with which he was unacquainted. They began to understand better the battered and mutilated state in which their own neat plans and policies finally reached the worker, after having been transmitted through an elaborate supervisory hierarchy. Also they began to understand better why the reports they received from their immediate subordinates as to what was happening at the front line, after having been transmitted through an elaborate supervisory hierarchy, did not quite coincide with what they learned from the interviewing program.

In short, they began to see that right before their eyes was occurring a very complicated phenomenon, a phenomenon which was very different from what it was represented to be in their blueprint plans. This complicated phenomenon was an intricate web of human relations bound together by a system of sentiments. Such a social structure is riddled with social routines which define our attitudes and feelings, our duties and obligations to one another. It tells us what kind of behavior is expected of us, as well as the kind of behavior we can expect from others.

Many industrial problems need to be redefined in terms of social structure. In the first place, we have to understand better the particular social structures of industry. Industrial organizations make for socially ordered, if not logical, living. In terms of social routines they control and regulate the behavior and the attitudes of the individuals within them. Not only do such organizations make for efficient social living; they also make for stability. Any serious disruption of them arouses feelings of insecurity among their members.

However, this respect for social structure in general should not blind us to the limitations of certain social structures in particular. Social structures not only make for stability; in some instances they make for red tape. They also make for difficulties in communication, difficulties in transmitting orders down the line as well as in obtaining accurate information up the line. There are certain types of structures which prevent the right kind of men from reaching the top rather than facilitating their progress. In other words, *the social structure of any particular company determines the kind of collaboration, the kind of people who will stay in the company, and the kind of people who will reach the top.*

CHAPTER IV

THE SOCIAL STRUCTURE OF INDUSTRY

TOO frequently the human activities of industry are conceived of as essentially economic. An industrial organization is assumed to be composed of a number of individuals entering into relations of contract for the promotion of their own individual economic interests. It is not easy to explain why this conception, which runs counter to everyday experience, should be so firmly entrenched in the minds of men and why it should be so difficult to eradicate. In many of the written decisions of management it lies as an implicit premise, unchallenged and absolute. Fortunately, many executives in action are wiser than their theories and often make decisions in terms of factors not strictly economic. Yet few of them when challenged can resist the temptation to rationalize their practices in terms of this oversimplified theory of human motivation.

SOCIAL BEHAVIOR

To say that a more adequate way of conceiving of the human activities of industry is to view them as essentially social brings up the question of what is meant by "social." There are few words more overworked or more shot through with different meanings. For some people the word "social" applies only to those activities enjoyed after work in the company of one's friends. It calls forth ideas of social clubs, social sets, or social circles, of people who seek diversion through association with others, and of activities pertaining essentially to the pleasure-seeking world. For others, it may bring to mind people who are sociable by nature and in habit and who have a disposition for coöperative relations with their fellow men. Those who are more serious or "socially minded" may immediately think of social problems, such as crime, suicide, and divorce, or the conditions and welfare of different groups within the community — the poor, the alien, the neglected, the maladjusted. Their thoughts then may run to social legislation, social work, social diseases, social hygiene, and social security. Another group of serious students may think of social theories or social questions pertaining to the fundamental relation between capital and labor.

But in speaking of social or socialized behavior I shall not be referring to any of these high abstractions in particular, but to far more simple matters. From experience we know that individuals interact and that the expression of that interaction is commonly recognized as social behavior. *Whenever a person is acting in accordance with the expectations and sentiments of some other person, or groups of persons, his behavior is social or socialized.* Such behavior, it is easy to see, can occur in a bread line just as well as at a fox hunt. It is manifested by the millionaire socialite owner of a factory as well as by his most lowly skilled worker. It occurs just as much at work as it does outside of working hours. In fact, there are few acts of men that are not social in the way in which I have defined the word.

CUSTOMARY OR ROUTINE WAYS OF BEHAVIOR

One can hardly speak of socialized behavior without understanding customary, traditional, or routine ways of doing things. Strangely enough, custom has never been considered a subject of great scientific importance. For any one scientific book describing the folkways and customs of any locality there can be found at least ten books about what behavior in general is or should be. Compared with the dignity of exploring the inner workings of the brain, the study of customary behavior is likely to be thought of as undignified and commonplace.

The reader would be bored if I should describe that mass of detailed behavior which goes to make up my daily existence. The facts about my shaving and washing before dressing in the morning, the articles of clothing I put on and the order in which I put them on, the kinds of foods I eat and when and how I eat them, the way in which the different objects on the table are arranged, the order in which the different members of my family sit — all this would probably soon elicit the comment, "So what? Roughly, everyone does the same things. These patterns of behavior which you so minutely describe are well-understood and recognized responses to rational or biological needs. Is there anything more to be said about them?"

In my opinion, there is. In the first place, it is a well-known fact that these routine patterns of behavior vary with different localities. We would all agree that coffee for breakfast and three meals a day are not universal routines of behavior. Yet, many of these routines are so close and fundamental to us that they lie outside the field of our conscious attention. As a result, we tend to identify our own particular local ways of behaving and thinking with behavior and thought in general. Our attention is directed to them only when we are brought into contact with groups whose customary ways of doing things are different from our own.

In the second place, these customary ways of doing things are frequently the occasion for the affirmation of our solidarity with groups. The family meal is more than an occasion for the satisfaction of biological needs. It also satisfies certain emotional needs of men. It is, for example, the occasion when the members of the family come together and when the father has an opportunity to see his children.

Now it can be seen that these customary ways of doing things constitute the framework within which the social life of groups is carried on. This framework is seldom completely coincident with biological needs. On biological grounds alone, a cup of hot water would be as good for me in the morning as a cup of coffee. A good case, in the name of science, could be made to the effect that some number other than three meals a day would be more appropriate to my sedentary way of living. Yet, were I to insist on such changes in family routines, it is probable that my wife would assume that something was wrong with me. I would be badgered with questions: "Aren't you feeling well? Don't you think you should see the doctor?" And, curiously enough, in spite of the fact that I should have science on my side, more often than not my wife would be right, not in sending me to the doctor but in feeling intuitively that my total disregard for the customary routines of behavior was symptomatic of a morbid preoccupation about my health. It is not entirely fortuitous that most neurotic ailments appear in connection with the breakdown of customary ways of doing things.

Socialized behavior, I have said, is behavior in accordance with the expectations and sentiments of others. Such behavior is expressed most often in terms of customary routines. These routines act as a sort of social cement. They bind men together in collaborative effort. Moreover, they change slowly and provide security for the individuals who perform them together.

ECONOMIC ASPECTS OF PRIMITIVE SOCIAL ORGANIZATION

Before looking at modern industry from the point of view of socialized behavior, I shall describe first the economic aspects of a more primitive type of society. By looking at a different culture we sometimes see more clearly certain uniformities of relationship that escape our attention when looking at our own.

Among the natives inhabiting a group of islands north and east of New Guinea, there exists a set of trade activities which has been interestingly described by Malinowski.[1] Round these

[1] B. Malinowski, *Argonauts of the Western Pacific* (London: G. Routledge & Sons, Ltd., 1932).

islands, which roughly are in the shape of a ring forming a closed circuit, two kinds of articles are constantly circulating; long necklaces of red shell travel about the islands always in a clockwise direction, and bracelets of white shell circulate always in the opposite direction. These articles are of no use to the natives except for ornamentation and are not used for this purpose to any extent. And yet these apparently worthless articles keep going round and round these islands. The natives of one island are continually giving gifts of red necklaces to the natives of another island on their clockwise side and receiving gifts of white bracelets in return. To their neighbors on their counterclockwise side, they are making gifts of white bracelets and receiving in return gifts of red necklaces.

This exchange of these two articles is known as the Kula. It takes place at definite times, in a definite manner, and between definitely prescribed partners. No Kula article remains in the hands of any one individual for any great length of time. At some future time and place it will be exchanged for some other article of equivalent prestige value. Each native knows just what these prestige value equivalences are, that is, for example, how many red necklaces of a particular kind are equivalent to a white bracelet of a particular kind. Every detail of the transaction is regulated by a set of traditional rules and conventions and is accompanied by elaborate public ceremonies. It would be irrelevant to describe in detail the rules and regulations of these ceremonial transactions; it is enough to say that they cover a complex of interrelated activities which are rooted in myth and backed by tradition. These Kula articles are prized very highly by the natives. Each necklace and bracelet has its own peculiar history and the natives spend much time in swapping stories about the individual fortunes or misfortunes of each article.

There are a number of other activities associated with the

Kula. Along with the Kula system the natives carry on ordinary trade. Articles actually to be used are bartered from one island to another. Moreover, to go on these Kula expeditions to islands which are often separated by hundreds of miles of water, it is necessary for the natives to build sea-going canoes. So it can be seen that what we would regard as important economic activities—trade and canoe building—are going on in these islands in association with the exchange of necklaces and bracelets. An outsider looking on might think that these were the really important activities and that the Kula proper was only a secondary phenomenon, an indirect stimulus encouraging the natives to sail and trade. I can imagine that a modern industrial engineer entrusted with the economic reorganization of these islands might say, "Let's stop these 'Kula-shines' and get down to the real business of trade and canoe building." And he might substitute more modern incentives to get the natives about their "real" business.

Now, strange as it may seem to our own ways of thinking and behaving, to the natives themselves the Kula proper is the primary and chief activity; trading and canoe building are activities secondary to it. From studying the behavior of the natives and all their customs, Malinowski found that "the Kula is in all respects the main aim: the dates are fixed, the preliminaries settled, the expeditions arranged, the social organisation determined, not with regard to trade, but with regard to Kula. On an expedition, the big ceremonial feast, held at the start, refers to the Kula; the final ceremony of reckoning and counting the spoil refers to Kula, not to the objects of trade obtained. Finally, the magic, which is one of the main factors of all the procedure, refers only to the Kula, and this applies even to a part of the magic carried out over the canoe. . . . The construction of the canoes is always carried on directly in connection with a Kula expedition."[2]

[2] Malinowski, p. 101.

The Kula, then, is more than a meaningless circulation of two worthless articles. It is a complex institution and as such plays a vital part in the lives of these savages. It is in this Kula setting that their productive activities gain meaning and significance, and to isolate these activities from this social setting is to give a completely erroneous and misleading picture of the economic life of these natives. Unthinking interference with a trading system such as this, which from our point of view may appear to be cumbersome and inefficient, would upset the entire social equilibrium and would rob the natives of those very social sentiments which provide an incentive to work. Yet very often by a failure to understand such social organizations, the white man deeply offends native belief and seriously affects capacity for work. The white man tends to divorce magic from work and is surprised when the suppression of one leads to inefficiency in the other.

This example of a primitive economic organization illustrates two points very clearly: In the first place, it shows that the forces which make collaboration possible among these natives are only in part economic; to a great extent they are essentially social and religious. Social motives, far more than expectations of economic gain, determine individual action. In the second place, these people are likely to assume that if the rules of the tribe imposed by tradition are rigidly upheld — that is, if all those ceremonials and rituals that play such an important role in maintaining the collaborative effort and unity of the group are seriously carried out — the economic problems will more or less take care of themselves.

Of course, this social philosophy could not be stated explicitly by any of the natives. If one were to talk to the older men of the tribe, however, one would find that most of their interest and attention is directed toward those matters pertaining to the social rather than to the economic organization of the group. Here, then, is a striking difference from the assumption of our civilization. *The primitive leader assumes that if he maintains the discipline imposed by tradition there will be few economic problems. Today we make the contrary assumption. We assume that if we understand intelligently the conditions necessary for the getting of raw materials and the technical production and distribution of goods, we need to give but little attention to the problems involved in collaborative effort; that is, the human problems of effective and meaningful association at work will take care of themselves.*

MODERN INDUSTRIAL ORGANIZATION

Now in stating this formulation I have oversimplified matters. There are, of course, certain individuals throughout the field of modern business who are giving attention to problems of human collaboration. It might even be argued that there are distinct groups of people — personnel organizations — who give their entire time to this problem. And yet if one looks carefully at these individuals or personnel organizations one is apt to find a strong tendency to separate the strictly technical problems of production and distribution from the human problems connected with work association. It would not be an exaggeration to say that the activities of most personnel organizations are largely based upon this very sharp separation of technical or economic matters from matters of human concern. Very seldom do such organizations act in an advisory capacity regarding technical practices of the company. From the economic viewpoint most personnel people are considered supernumeraries. Most of their duties are concerned with the routine carrying out of policies that have been settled by other groups or with settling as best they can human problems that have already been created. There is a tendency in modern industrial organization to separate the economic function from all the social interrelations and to believe that in the settlement of economic problems it is not necessary to consider any other aspect of human organization. The following are concrete examples from factory situations.

Example No. 1

A company in the process of reorganization found that it had on its hands approximately 200 people whose jobs had been so greatly simplified that their highly developed skill was no longer required. Fortunately, the company was then enjoying renewed business activity so that it was possible to reabsorb these people in other parts of the plant. The executives of the company felt that this problem could be solved by transferring these employees to new jobs whenever vacancies occurred in other types of work. At the same time management insisted that there should be no diminution in the "take-home." Workers should be transferred only to jobs on which they could earn as much money as they had been able to earn on their old jobs.

Now it can be seen that the logic of management was very simple. It assumed that inasmuch as the worker was primarily interested in the "take-home," any transference to another job, regardless of its nature, in which the weekly pay was not affected would be satisfactory to the employee. This logic holds in many instances primarily because two jobs whose earnings are more or less the same carry with them more or less the same social status in the company. In this particular case, however, this assumption did not hold. It happened that many of the jobs which had been affected by the reorganization were, in terms of the attitudes of the employees toward them, "superior" to those to which they were being asked to transfer. The reorganization meant transferring stock assemblers and storeroom keepers to simple machine operations or assembly work. The results were not satisfactory. Many employees who were given a choice of new jobs did not care to accept. Instead they preferred to stay on their existing jobs until conditions made it imperative to transfer, even though staying involved the risk of diminished earnings.

Example No. 2

Many times management makes certain changes based upon logical and economic considerations and then finds that the human interrelations which were also affected by the change create new and difficult problems. Let me take, for example, a company in which the primary manufacturing activities were divided into six functional units such as operation, inspection, production, etc. Each of these functional units had its own hierarchy of authority and interacted with the other functional units only at certain specified points in the manufacturing process. Although this type of organization secured excellent vertical control within each function, there still existed the difficulty of coördinating the activities of the various functions. This lack of coördination, particularly at the lower levels, resulted in manufacturing inefficiency. To obviate this difficulty, it became necessary to reorganize the company on new lines. A number of different shops were set up, the activities of each centering around a particular product which it manufactured from start to finish. Under this new plan each shop had its own inspection and production people, who were now expected to report to supervisors in the operating line organization. Logically, this new setup should produce the desired effect of coördination of functions and probably in time will do so. But at present the company is finding that it is much easier to coördinate these logical functions on paper than to coördinate the people carrying them out. It is easier to change the logical basis of organization than to change the routine human sentiments that are being violated by the reorganization.

Immediately following this reorganization, the production and inspection people, the former in particular, began to register many complaints. They found the lighting conditions in their new surroundings faulty; they did not like the common washrooms. They found fault with the lockers. Some of them went to extreme lengths in registering their dissatisfaction. One employee, for instance, refused to use the washroom on the floor where he worked and laboriously climbed several stories to use a washroom for office employees. But far more serious were the organizational difficulties that developed. There was a tendency for production clerks to short-circuit the new formal lines of authority. Instead of reporting directly to their immediate superiors — the operating supervisors — they were likely to go to production supervisors up the line.

An explanation of this situation may be found in the fact that the new organization had broken down the sharp distinction between office people and shop people that had existed under the old arrangement. In the old organization, production clerks had regarded themselves as office people. Their feeling of superiority to shop people was not merely a fanciful whim, for, although there were no written statements by the company to this effect, in all the minor distinctions and privileges which differentiated office people from shop people — lockers and washroom facilities, for example — production people were socially identified with office people. Under the new organization they felt that their status had been jeopardized; in terms of the customary interhuman relations they felt they had been demoted. Their complaints were an expression of this disruption in the social equilibrium to which they had become accustomed.

Example No. 3

The foundry department of a manufacturing concern employed some fifty men who were almost all highly skilled craftsmen and long-service employees. These workers prided themselves on their traditions and clung to certain privileges, such as smoking on the job, which were denied to other employees in the factory. According to the nature of their work, the foundry workers were differentiated into four groups. These job groups, according to the foundrymen themselves, were not of equal importance. Each had its own social values and its own rank in the social scale. One of these groups was dominant, and in this group three or four members rigidly controlled the rest.

About three or four years ago, in line with its general policy, the company put all the foundry employees on group piecework. Up to this time they had been on straight piecework. Management felt that, under group piecework, earnings could be distributed more equitably and that such an arrangement would divide among all the employees the responsibility for turning out a satisfactory product and for reducing the amount of scrap due to defective castings. Such was the logic of what should happen. What actually happened was something quite different. Total output, instead of increasing, went down. The problem of scrap, instead of being solved, tended to reappear and complicate other issues. The iron molders felt they were not getting what they earned. Those operators with high outputs felt they were carrying the less efficient men. Molders did not see why they should be penalized for parts that were broken by the chippers and grinders. Some of the men who had previously earned about $1.00 an hour now earned about $.75 an hour; this in spite of the fact that the new rates under the group payment plan were not in any way "tighter" than the old rates under straight piecework.

So management was faced with the problem of disentangling itself from the human complications of its own logic. The situation was far more complex than my oversimplified account has suggested. In essence, however, it was a situation of extreme resistance to a change introduced by management which failed to take into account the social sentiments of the foundrymen. To the foundry employees there were four different social groups — four different ways of life — which, under the new wage payment system, were no longer recognized. The foundry employees never ceased to petition management to put them back on straight piecework or, failing this, to divide them, at least for the purpose of payment, into the four natural job groups. However, for technical reasons, management found it impossible to make either of these two moves. As a result, the employees tried to force the hand of management by restricting output even at the expense of lowered individual earnings.

Example No. 4

Suggestion plans, according to the general logic of management, are intended to promote constructive thinking and coöperation of employees. In one company such a system was introduced. The method of administration was very simple. Suggestions handed in by the employees were considered by a committee, and suitable awards were made for accepted suggestions. Management believed that notice of these awards should be posted publicly on the bulletin boards in order to stimulate submission of suggestions and give the suggesters full recognition. However, the public posting of awards met with increasing dissatisfaction on the part of the workers. If a worker submitted a suggestion that either eliminated an operation, or so simplified or changed a work routine that rate revision was necessary, a great deal of social pressure was put on this operator by his fellow workers. Often a foreman discriminated against a worker who turned in a suggestion that improved a process for which the foreman himself was responsible. He tended to interpret such a suggestion as criticism of his work and either penalized the worker or tried to rearrange the process in such a way that the suggestion was no longer of value. Many disputes arose as to the distribution of the "windfall" when an award was made public. If the suggester owed money, claimants would appear and ask the company to effect a settlement. For these reasons, management finally had to publish awards by code number only, thereby nullifying in part the original intention of the plan. Management's logical method of promoting collaboration had failed to take into account other important aspects of this human organization.

THE SOCIAL ORGANIZATION OF INDUSTRY

These examples show that industry has a social organization which cannot be treated independently from the technical problems of economic organization. An industrial organization is more than a plurality of individuals acting only with regard to their own economic interests. These individuals also have feelings and sentiments toward one another, and in their daily associations together they tend to build up routine patterns of interaction. Most of the individuals who live among these patterns come to accept them as obvious and necessary truths and to react as they dictate.

If one looks at a factory situation, for example, one finds individuals and groups of people associated together at work, acting in certain accepted and prescribed ways toward one another. There is not complete homogeneity of behavior between individuals or between one group of individuals and another, but rather there are differences of behavior expressing differences in social relationship. Individuals conscious of their membership in certain groups are reacting in certain accepted ways to other individuals representing another group. Behavior varies according to these stereotyped conceptions of relationship. The worker, for example, behaves toward his foreman in one way, toward his first-line supervisor in another way, and toward his fellow worker in still another. People holding the rank of inspectors expect a certain kind of behavior from the operators; the operators from the inspectors. Now these relationships, as we all know from everyday experience, are finely shaded and sometimes become very complicated. When a person is in the presence of his boss alone, he acts quite differently from the way he acts when his boss's boss is also present. Likewise his boss acts toward him alone quite differently from the way he behaves when his own boss is also there. These subtle nuances of relationship are so much a part of our everyday life that they are commonplace. We take them for granted. We hardly realize the vast amount of social conditioning that has taken place in order that we can maneuver ourselves gracefully through the intricacies of these finely shaded social distinctions. We only pay attention to them when we blunder into new social situations where our past social training prevents us from making the necessary delicate interpretation of a given social signal and hence brings forth the socially wrong response.

In the factory, as in any social milieu, a process of social evaluation is constantly at work. From this process distinctions of good, bad, inferior, superior, etc., arise. This process of evaluation is carried on with simple and ready generalizations by means of which values become attached to individuals and to groups performing certain tasks and operations. It assigns to a group of individuals performing such and such a task a particular rank in the established prestige scale. Each work group becomes a carrier of social value. In industry, with its extreme diversity of occupations, there are a number of such groupings. Any noticeable similarity or difference, not only in occupation but also in age, sex, and nationality, can serve as a basis of social classification, as for example the married woman, the old-timer, the white-collared or clerical worker, the foreign element. Each of these groups too has its own value system.

Now the patterns of interaction that arise between individuals or between different groups can be graded according to the degree of intimacy involved in a relationship. Grades of intimacy or understanding can be arranged on a scale and expressed in terms of social distance. Social distance measures differences of sentiment and interest which separate individuals or groups from one another. Between the president of a company and the elevator operator, there is considerable social distance; more, for example, than between the foreman and the bench worker. Social distance is to social organization what physical distance is to physical space. However, physical and social distance do not necessarily coincide. Two people may be physically near but socially distant.

Just as each employee has a particular physical location, so he has a particular social place in the total social organization. But this place is not so rigidly fixed as in a caste system. In any factory there is considerable social mobility or movement. Movement can occur in two ways: The individual may pass from one occupation to another occupation higher up in the prestige scale. Or the prestige scale itself may change. It is obvious that these scales of value are never completely accepted by all the groups in the social environment. The shop worker does not quite see why the office worker, for example, should have shorter hours of work than he has. Or the newcomer whose efficiency on a particular job is about the same but whose hourly rate is less than that of some old-timer wonders why service should count so much. The management group, in turn, from the security of its social elevation, does not understand what all the fuss is about. Advocates of a different social scale, therefore, are constantly trying to upset the existing social equilibrium and establish the supremacy of their own scale.

Any person who has achieved a certain rank in the prestige scale regards anything, real or imaginary, which tends to alter his status adversely as something unfair or unjust. It can be seen that any move on the part of the company may alter the existing social equilibrium to which the employee has grown accustomed and by means of which his status is defined. Immediately this disruption will be expressed in sentiments of resistance to the real or imagined alterations in the social equilibrium. In the case of the complaints of the production people previously given we have a good example of this phenomenon.

THE PROBLEM OF COMMUNICATION

In the technical organization of most companies there is very little explicit recognition given to these social distinctions. The blueprint organization plans of a company show the functional relations between working units, but they do not express these distinctions of social distance, movement, or equilibrium. This hierarchy of prestige values, which tends to make the work of men more important than the work of women, the work of clerks more important than the work at the bench, has no meaning for the technical organization. Nor does a blueprint plan show the primary groups, that is, those groups enjoying daily face-to-face relations. Logical lines of vertical and horizontal coördination of functions replace the actually existing patterns of interaction between people of different social places. From a technical standpoint, social place has no existence; only physical space exists. In place of all the sentiments of value residing in the social organization by means of which individuals and groups of individuals are differentiated, ordered, and integrated, there is substituted the logic of efficiency. Now it can be seen that this failure to recognize explicitly these human interrelations has certain consequences.

For example, the problem of communication is very important in the effective integration of any group or of a group of groups, of which industry is composed. Successful communication between individuals depends upon something more than a common language, a common set of words. People and groups with different experiences and social places, although having in common many of the same words, may vary widely in mental attitudes. These differences in modes of thought and ways of viewing things may make communication in some instances almost impossible. The trained expert with his precise and logical vocabulary has difficulty in communicating with the layman. The customary ways of thinking of the skilled toolmaker, for example, are quite different from those of the non-machine minded unskilled worker. They differ also from those of the engineer, the accountant, the marketing expert, the executive, or the administrator. As it is commonly expressed, people with different ways of thinking do not "get" each other.

If there is to be successful communication between the top and bottom of an industrial organization, these differences in modes of thought must be more clearly recognized. The same symbol does not necessarily have the same referent for different groups. Most symbols not only point out something, they also convey certain emotions. There is no better example than the case of the language of efficiency. The top of the organization is trying to communicate with the bottom in terms of the logical jargon and cold discriminations of the technical specialist, the engineer, the accountant, etc. The bottom of the organization, in turn, is trying to communicate with the top through its own peculiar language of social sentiments and feelings. Neither side understands the other very well. To the bottom the precise language of efficiency, instead of transmitting understanding, sometimes conveys feelings of dismay and insecurity. The bottom, in turn, instead of transmitting successfully its fears of social dislocation, conveys to the top emotional expressions of petty grievances and excessive demands.

The following situation is an example of what I mean. A company found it advisable to reduce the hourly rates of a number of long-service employees. This move was made not with the idea of reducing labor costs, but primarily with motives of "fairness and justice" in mind. It happened that the company had been left after the depression with a number of long-service people whose hourly rates were "out of line" with the grades of work they were doing. When business picked up and new employees were hired at hourly rates comparable to the grades of work to which they were assigned, and put into work groups with these longer-service people under the group payment plan, a situation to the disadvantage of the younger and newer men was created. In fairness to these new men, management felt something should be done. Clearly, the executives of the company had human values in mind when making this change. The purpose of their plan was to redistribute more equitably the total earnings of a group piecework department among its individual members. But here is the curious part of the story. When the company put in this change, it explained the move to the employees concerned in terms of the language of efficiency. The employees' response to this move was bitter and voluble. The more management tried to explain its reasons for making this change, the more resistance it met. Finally, one executive in conference with the employee representatives saw what had happened. The company had always had a policy favorable to its long-service employees. With this move, the long-service employees felt that the company had changed its policy with regard to them. It seemed to them that efficiency only, not service, now counted in the company. When the executive was able to reassure the employees that this move in no way had changed the basic company policy toward seniority, that long service was still valued and would be rewarded by certain considerations and privileges, the disturbance died down. The employees affected were satisfied to accept the change as long as the social values attaching to long service, which the company had upheld, had not been changed.

CONCLUSION

In conclusion, let me review briefly the points that I have made:

(1) Without misunderstanding, no particular economic activity can be torn apart from its surrounding social fabric and treated as a thing in itself. In the trade activities of the natives of the Melanesian Archipelago, for example, the economic functions of trade and canoe building cannot be adequately understood apart from the background of the Kula, a set of beliefs and attitudes expressing their social organization.

(2) Modern management tends to subsume the problems of group collaboration under the technical problems of production and efficiency. As a result, collaboration is conceived of as a logical contrivance for getting people to work together by appealing primarily to their individual economic interests.

(3) However, modern industry is built up of a number of small working groups. Between the individuals within these groups and between individuals of different groups, there exist patterns of behavior which are expressing differences in social relationship. Each job has its own social values and its rank in the social scale.

(4) Each industrial concern has a social as well as a physical structure. Each employee not only has a physical place but he also has a social place in the factory. Any technical change on the part of management may therefore affect not only the physical but also the social location of an individual or group of employees. This fear of social dislocation is likely to be a constant threat to the social security of different individuals and groups of individuals within the industry.

(5) The failure on the part of management to understand explicitly its social structure means that it often mistakes logical coördination for social integration. This confusion interferes

with successful communication up and down the line as well as between different groups within the industry.

As I have said before, primitive man attaches primary importance to the social organization of the group; his economic life is completely subservient to it. Primitive belief assumes that by strict upholding of the tribal customs expressing social organization it can meet the exigencies of nature — a food shortage or drought, for example. Modern belief, on the other hand, assumes that by the efficient production and distribution of goods, it can fulfill the demands of human nature. As a result we have the goods but the natives have the morale.

It is needless to point out that neither position is tenable. However, it is much easier to see the absurdity of primitive belief than to see the absurdity of our own. It seems obvious to our logical ways of thinking that no ritualistic performance of certain ceremonials can bring forth the rain that is necessary for the successful growing of crops. It is less obvious that the application of science to agriculture does not in itself provide the basis for meaningful human association at work.

CHAPTER V

A DISINTERESTED OBSERVER LOOKS AT INDUSTRY

MANY practical problems of industry involve phenomena in which interaction between persons is an important factor. Facts of social behavior are likely to be considered simple and obvious, and sometimes even trivial. Regardless, however, of how simple or trivial such facts may appear to us under the influence of our sentiments, their importance lies in what we can do with them and not in how we feel about them. Moreover, there is a tendency to ignore and forget the simple and obvious when it is most important to remember it.

Facts of social behavior are obtained from the study of concrete cases. In an industrial concern they come from firsthand observation of people at work. For the untrained person, such observations are difficult because interactions between persons more often than not are expressed in terms of norms which the observer takes for granted. Only variations from these norms attract his attention; the norms themselves remain unnoticed. However, instead of trying to acquaint the reader in a systematic manner with this class of phenomena involving interaction between persons, it may be more simple if we first look at these phenomena directly. With this in mind, therefore, let us plan a tour of observation through industry. Because of our limited time, this tour must necessarily be restricted to a few spots, but it will be well to remember that these spots have not been selected because there is anything particularly dramatic to be seen there. We shall not be looking for dirt in either the literal or the figurative sense. Rather, these spots have been chosen because it is hoped they will evoke in the reader a feeling of familiarity. They will have a homely quality about them.

THE OBSERVER'S BACKGROUND AND VIEWPOINT

On this tour we shall be accompanied by a disinterested observer of social behavior who will keep us in touch with the kinds of things he is observing, as well as the questions and exclamations that accompany his reactions to those things he sees and hears. Inasmuch as this observer will be looking at his data from a certain point of view and with a certain background of experience, it may be well first to state what these are. First, he is unacquainted with the particular social behavior that he will be describing to us. Instead of handicapping him, this will enable him to see with fresh eyes those things which our eyes have grown so accustomed to seeing that, in a sense, we no longer see them. We take them for granted.

Secondly, he has studied in a serious and careful manner, and from a functional viewpoint, the social organization of some culture groups, different, of course, from our own. "From a functional viewpoint" means that he has studied the social institutions of people as something intrinsically related to, and not as something apart from, the people who participate in these institutions. He has been interested in the "meaning" or "function" which their institutionalized or customary ways of behavior have for them. He has observed the social interactions of people in their everyday life, when at work and at play, within and without the family, at big public ceremonial occasions, at times of peace and at times of crisis. He has been interested in the objects, myths, and beliefs which are associated with their activities. For example, at any ceremonial occasion, he has been trained to observe the people who participate, whether men or women, young or old; the manner in which each of these groups participates; and the objects, myths, and beliefs which are associated with the particular occasion. From this sort of data, obtained by observation and interviewing, he has sought for the sentiments and attitudes which regulate the behavior of people toward one another.[1]

Thirdly, the observer has found it useful in his work to take a certain point of view toward the words and symbols used by his informants. He has learned from experience the misunderstanding that may arise from confusing or identifying verbal with nonverbal phenomena, and the need for keeping these two levels of behavior clearly differentiated. The tendency to confuse words with the things they represent he has found one of the most difficult and persistent errors against which to guard himself. In his work, therefore, he is constantly looking for the referents of the symbols used by his informants, that is, for what these symbols stand in the actual social life of the people he is studying. According to the observer's viewpoint, what a symbol stands for or what a word refers to in experience is not itself a word. Therefore, in his opinion it would not help him very much to go to a dictionary for the meaning of a word used by his informants. What a dictionary does is to substitute one set of symbols for another set of symbols. The observer, however, is interested in the objects and events, and particularly those events involving human interaction, to which these words refer. For him the referents of symbols are to be found in the world of experience and not in a dictionary.

In terms of our culture, then, our observer will be socially

[1] Within sociology and anthropology today a controversy still exists between the "historical" and the "functional" approach. With this controversy the observer is not concerned. It is his belief that any approach is neither true nor false but only more or less convenient or useful for certain purposes. Moreover, its utility for certain purposes cannot be decided *a priori*. Its utility can only be decided after the method has been used. "The eye of the artist or poet looking at the human body is different from the eye of the physician looking for pathological symptoms. Neither one has the 'true' nor the 'false' view of the body. The physician, however, is the better person when therapy rather than decoration is demanded." (Thurman W. Arnold, *The Symbols of Government*, New Haven: Yale University Press, 1935, p. 30.)

dumb but intelligent. He will be socially dumb in the sense that he does not know enough to take his hat off to a woman acquaintance when passing her in the street, but intelligent in the sense that he will be observant enough to note such behavior on the part of men toward women in the group which he is studying.

THE OBSERVER MEETS AN ECONOMIST AND SOME BUSINESS LEADERS

Thus our observer comes to these shores, having read books on the industrial civilization he has come to observe, but having had no firsthand acquaintance with it. As he sails into New York harbor and views with interest the skyline of lower Manhattan, a group of reporters are interviewing him about his plans. "It is my understanding," he says, "that there are a group of people in this society, called 'economists,' who have charted out the way businessmen behave, or at least should behave for their own interests, and it is to one of these economists that I should like to talk first before I interview businessmen, their representatives, and employees." Accordingly, a tour is arranged for the observer which includes meeting an economist and then some business leaders. Afterwards he will visit a large industrial plant where he will have an opportunity to talk to the general manager, as well as to his staff of specialists, junior supervisors, and workers.

According to schedule, we find him first talking to an economist who is a member of one of the leading universities in the community. They are discussing the question of labor supply and its relation to wage differentials. The economist is speaking. "There is a tendency," he says, "for industries using considerable unskilled help to move from communities where labor is high to those communities where they can get their labor more cheaply, thereby reducing their labor cost and increasing their profit." The economist mentions certain businessmen who, because they have failed to take heed of this principle, have gone out of business. Although the economist does not say so explicitly, there is an implication throughout the discussion that when businessmen do not behave in accordance with their best interests it is largely because they do not know what their best interests are and have failed to go to the universities to find out. "Businessmen," continues the economist, "are not sufficiently versed in simple economic principles." Throughout the conversation there recur such phrases as "all things being equal," "in the main," "in general," which the observer notices and writes down in his field notes after the interview. That a question is beginning to be formulated in his mind can be detected by some of the remarks he puts down in his notebook, such as: "Test economist's hypotheses; what are the referents for such expressions as 'in the main,' 'in general,' 'all things being equal'; what function do they fulfill for the economist who uses them?"[2]

Armed with hypotheses which he can test, the observer goes into the community. He begins to listen to and observe the behavior of Business Leader 1, Business Leader 2, Business Leader 3, etc., engaged in both large and small enterprises. He finds that although some businessmen in some events behave the way the economist said they behave, or should behave, these same men on other occasions do not. Some businessmen act in terms of a strict economic logic on more occasions than do others. And, moreover, he finds that of the businessmen who on most occasions behave with regard to economic "principles," some are successful and some are not. And the same thing holds for businessmen who do not behave strictly according to economic "principles," for some of these are successful

[2] From these particular statements of a particular economist the reader should draw no conclusions about the thinking of all economists in general. The observer is aware that this particular economist may not be representative of his class. Whether he is or is not is irrelevant to the observer's immediate purposes. The economist's statements have provided him with a "lead" for observing the concrete behavior of business leaders.

and some are not. So the observer writes down in his notebook: "Things do not seem to be 'all equal,' 'in the main,' or 'in general.' Economist may have missed important variable. Better investigate further." [3]

Our observer begins to investigate these four groups of businessmen: (1) those who act more often with regard to economic "principles"; (2) those who act less often with regard to economic "principles"; and within each of these groups (3) those who are considered to be successful; (4) those who are not. He interviews industrialists from each of these groups, and gradually a uniformity seems to emerge. Tentatively he states it something like this: "It looks as if some business leaders who do not behave on some important occasions strictly according to economic 'principles' are members of the community in which their factory is located. In their interviews they express such sentiments as 'feelings of social obligation and responsibility to the community in which they are living.' On some occasions these sentiments influence their decisions. Some of those who are successful have little or no labor trouble. On the other hand, some business leaders who act more often in accordance with economic 'principles' seem to be living in communities quite geographically separate from where their factories are located. In their interviews they talk about 'costs,'

[3] Because some economic theories have little value in enabling one to predict any concrete event, anywhere and at any time, the reader should not draw any adverse conclusion about the utility of such theories for economic thought. In physics, Newton's theory of the tides offers a good example. From this theory no one has been able to deduce what the tide will be anywhere and at any time. However, most physicists are aware of the limitations of this theory. They do not expect it to do something for which it is not intended. For an interesting discussion of this question, read V. Pareto, *The Mind and Society* (New York: Harcourt, Brace and Company, 1935), vol. III, p. 1191. Also cf. Frank Knight's statement: "It [theoretical economics] can tell us little in the concrete and its chief function is negative — to offset as far as possible the stupid theorizing of the man in the street." — "The Limitations of Scientific Method in Economics" in *The Trend of Economics*, edited by R. G. Tugwell (New York: Alfred A. Knopf, 1924), p. 267.

'profits,' and similar things about which the economist had also expounded at great length. Some of these industrialists seem to have considerable labor trouble."[4]

THE OBSERVER ENTERS A FACTORY AND MEETS A GENERAL MANAGER

We next find the observer in the office of the general manager of a large industrial enterprise. The latter is poring over something which is to be a never-ending source of astonishment and mystery to the observer — an organization chart. The general manager's desk, which the observer had noticed when he entered the room was free of all objects except a telephone and a calendar pad, is now littered with blue charts which show the formal relations each person in the company is supposed to have to those people who work for him as well as to those people for whom he works. He is being initiated by the general manager into such mysteries as "staff and line," "centralization and decentralization of functions," "centralization and decentralization of authority," "straight-line production," "functional as opposed to product-shop organization."

Although our observer's mind is in a whirl over all these new terms, he is still capable of making two simple observa-

[4] This generalization is to be viewed as a very first and rough approximation which will require modification as the observer collects more facts. Its importance to the observer lies in directing his attention roughly to the area where the missing variables may be found in order to describe the concrete behavior of businessmen.

Moreover, in this generalization nothing is being suggested or implied about the utility to society of the behavior of either kind of businessman mentioned above. That an economic belief or doctrine does not coincide with experimental fact has nothing to say about its social utility. According to the observer, the social utility of any doctrine or fiction is a matter for further investigation. But with the interesting but difficult question about the social utility of certain economic doctrines, the observer is not now concerned. He is only interested in the discovery that the abstractions of the economist are telling him little in the concrete. Inasmuch as his object is to study cases of human behavior, he can now go ahead with his observations, without the haunting fear that his job of describing such behavior has already been done.

tions: (1) The people at the top of the organization, including the person to whom he is talking, appear to be separated by many steps from the people at the bottom of the organization. (2) Although every place on the organization chart has a label attached to it, the labels at the top and middle of the chart refer to single persons, whereas the labels at the bottom, such as "workers," "clerks," etc., refer to groups of persons. These observations raise three questions in the observer's mind, so he asks the general manager: (1) Do the people at the bottom of the organization have any difficulty in understanding the economic and logical objectives of the people at the top? (2) Do the people at the top have difficulty in understanding the way the people at the bottom feel? (3) Although this chart shows how management is organized, how are all the people labeled "workers" (who, he understands, constitute two-thirds of the population) organized?

The last question seems to touch off something in the general manager's preoccupations, for he answers the last question first. He explains to the observer, with a note of pride in his voice, that his workers are "unorganized." "Unorganized!" repeats the observer, with a touch of astonishment in his voice. "But how is that possible? Don't they have any social relations with their fellow workers and supervisors?" "I said 'unorganized,' not 'disorganized,'" says the general manager. "I heard you the first time," thinks the observer, writing in his notebook. He does not pursue the subject, for he remembers the precept of his former teachers, "Never dispute about words," and he instinctively realizes from the tone of the general manager's voice that although they are using the same words they are not referring to the same things.[5]

[5] It is not the observer's opinion that any general manager would confuse his organization chart (a map) with his organization (the territory, i.e., referent). But, after having talked with the economist, he is wondering if there may not be a more general confusion between the way an organization is logically and technically represented to be (a map, i.e., symbol system) and

The conversation shifts to the other questions. The general manager talks about his staff of technical experts. He has statisticians and accountants, who provide him with certain "control figures" through which he keeps his fingers on the pulse of things. He has specialists who help to "standardize" and make more "efficient" his plant operations and practices. There are people on his staff whose job it is to see that his workers get paid wages that are at least as much as, if not higher than, the wages being paid in the community for comparable work. There are specialists who see to it that the men are being selected and trained for those jobs which are best suited to their native endowment and capacity. Moreover, the supervisory staff is trained to keep him informed of the problems that occur on the line. "But sometimes," the general manager confesses, "I feel singularly out of touch with the situation in spite of all these important bits of paper that pass over my desk and in spite of the many conferences I have with my staff of specialists, and so occasionally I take a walk through the shops." He complains that the workers do not understand many of the policies and practices of the company, and he deplores their failure to appreciate better the economic and technical purposes of the company. He thinks that if only the workers could be kept more fully informed about the policies of the company, the major source of labor discontent would be eliminated. The general manager advises the observer to talk to some of his specialists.[6]

---

the way it is actually organized (the territory, i.e., referent), and he is interested to find out what individuals or groups of individuals are more likely to manifest this confusion. He will also have this question in mind, therefore, when interviewing other representatives and employees of the company.

[6] In talking to the general manager, the observer is aware that in many successful executives and administrators speech and action do not necessarily coincide. There are some administrators who hold no explicit theories about administration and yet are very successful. There are some successful administrators whose theories of administration do not coincide with their actual

THE OBSERVER INTERVIEWS SOME TECHNICAL SPECIALISTS

During the next few days our observer spends most of his time talking to different technical experts, some of whom report directly to the general manager and some of whom report to the general manager's subordinates down the line, his superintendents and general foremen. These experts include plant engineers, maintenance engineers, safety engineers, motion economy engineers, production engineers, inspectors, wage incentive system experts, cost accountants, and industrial relations people of one kind and another. The observer notes that certain titles which he has seen in books, such as "efficiency engineer," "time study engineer," "rate setter," are missing and he wonders if functions are being performed under the new titles that are the same, or different, from those performed under the old labels.

It would take too long to tell about the conversations which our observer has with these different people and the many charts and diagrams they use to describe and explain their work. He makes a number of observations, which he jots down in his notebook:

(1) Each specialist has a set of logically interrelated activities or functions to fulfill.

(2) Each specialist tends to see the total organization from the point of view of his own specialty.

(3) The function of coördinating the functions of these different specialists is not explicitly the function of any one of these specialists but of a line executive.

(4) Most of the specialists are experimentally minded and technically trained and talk a great deal about "efficiency."

(5) The word "efficiency" is used in at least five different ways, two of which are rather vague and not clearly differentiated: (a) Sometimes, when talking about a machine, it is used in its technical sense, as the relation between input and output; (b) sometimes, when talking about

---

behavior. There are some unsuccessful administrators who cannot apply what they theoretically know to be sound.

a manufacturing process or operation, it is used to refer to relative unit cost; (c) sometimes, when talking about a worker, it is used to refer to a worker's production or output in relation to a certain standard of performance; (d) sometimes, its referent becomes more vague, and it is used as practically synonymous with "logical coördination of functions"; (e) sometimes, it is used in the sense of "morale" or "social integration."

(6) Some of the activities of these specialists tend to make for originality and change in the organization, particularly at the bottom.

(7) Many of the plans and systems which these specialists devise are intended to help the workers; for example, the wage incentive system is designed to assist the worker in earning a wage proportional to his effort.

(8) Some of these plans are based on the assumption that the worker is primarily motivated by his economic interest.

(9) Most of the specialists come from a stratum of the community different from that of the workers and lower-ranking supervisors. On the whole, they have more education and training than the workers and lower-ranking supervisors. Many of them have a better logical training than they have training or experience in dealing with people; the opposite is more likely to be true of the lower-ranking supervisors.

(10) Some of the specialists tend to move into the management or executive group as they become older and more experienced.

(11) Some of the specialists have more prestige and authority to initiate action than others.

(12) Some of the staff specialists have administrative as well as advisory functions. At times, they originate action directly on the line, not only by devising new systems but by seeing that they are carried through.

(13) Each staff specialist has relations not only with his immediate superiors and subordinates, as shown on the blueprint chart, but also with other staff specialists, supervisors, and workers.

(14) Among these specialists there exist certain codes of behavior which define their relations to one another and to other groups in the organization. Although their behavior toward the problems they are solving is logico-experimental, their relations to one another are, for the most part, socially determined.[7]

[7] While reading these observations, the reader should remember that the observer is looking at an establishment employing a large number of people where "principles" of scientific management have been applied. Some of these observations may not apply to smaller and less highly "rationalized" concerns.

So much for his observations. Let us now look at some of the questions he puts down in his notebook:

(1) Does friction arise between these different specialists, and, if so, who handles these frictions and how?

(2) What may be the feeling on the part of those groups in the organization, particularly the foremen and the workers, who have to accommodate themselves to the changes these specialists initiate?

(3) Do the workers see these systems designed to further their economic interests as the creators of these systems see them, that is, as logical schemes which the workers can use for their own advantage?

(4) Do many workers or lower-ranking supervisors move up through the organization by means of staff jobs? Or has this path of mobility been effectively blocked for them?

(5) Have the actually existing patterns of interaction among these specialists and between them and other groups in the organization ever been studied?

(6) What might be the effect on the social organization of the company if many experimentally minded people were moved to the top and were put in charge of its economic destiny? [8]

THE OBSERVER LOOKS AT WORKING CONDITIONS

Our observer spends the next few days visiting the various shops and offices. He realizes that he has been listening to a great deal. He has listened to what people wanted to tell him, to what they did not want to tell him, and to what they could not tell him. Things they could not tell him were those assumptions which underlay everything they said but were not themselves expressed. From members of management and from their staff specialists he has heard how they and other people are supposed to behave. It has been written indelibly in his memory and his notebook that this behavior has something

[8] The observer is interested in the concrete. The answers to these questions, therefore, would not necessarily be the same for all industrial establishments, large and small, at any time and at any place. According to the observer, they are an interesting set of questions for any large-scale concern to ask itself. Any generalizations about modern industry in terms of these questions can come only from a number of studies of concrete cases.

to do with "efficiency," but now he feels that the time has come to observe a little social behavior and interaction in the raw. In his previous studies he had found it a good practice to differentiate clearly the way people say they behave, or explain their behavior, from the way they actually do behave.

The observer had found it enlightening in his other studies to look for "contexts of situation," that is, to look for the objects and symbols that are associated with certain kinds of human behavior and interaction. Only in this way had he been able to learn what certain objects and symbols meant to the people who used them. Instead of listening only to what people said about certain objects and symbols, he had been trained to note in what events involving human interaction they occurred. How did people use them? How did they behave toward them? In such contexts he was better able to see what they meant.

From this point of view the observer begins to look at various objects in industry which are associated with the behavior of people. He lcoks first at those objects on which the people are supposed to do their work, and he notes that for certain groups of people in the organization they are called "benches" and for other groups they are called "desks." He looks more carefully at the objects called desks and sees that there are two different kinds: single-pedestal desks and double-pedestal desks. He notes that when there is interaction between the occupant of a single-pedestal desk and the occupant of a double-pedestal desk, the occupant of the single-pedestal desk is the one who walks most often to the occupant of the double-pedestal desk. Although some people who sit at double-pedestal desks rationalize the size of a person's desk in terms of need and efficient use, there seems to be, in fact, an almost inverse correlation between the size of a person's desk and the technical need for that size. The less technical need for a large desk a person has, the bigger it seems to become. The observer notes a simple uniformity: The size of a person's desk is also related to the position or status he holds in the organization. "The bigger the 'shot,' the bigger the desk" is the way the observer expresses this in his notebook.

Our observer investigates the significance of many objects in this way. For example, he notes that there are certain people who use cloth towels, certain people who use paper towels, and certain people who are not provided with any towels at all. Pencils, tools, fixtures, pictures, water bottles, smoke, fumes, noise, dirt, rest periods, hourly rates, methods of payment, hours of work, and many other things, all called "plant conditions," are examined in this manner. Gradually the observer becomes acquainted with those objects which, because of their association in certain events involving human interactions, have or have not become symbols of status in the organization.[9]

In making these observations, the observer raises this question: There are, of course, certain people in an industrial organization, the general manager for instance, who are so uniquely differentiated from everyone else that were they deprived of one little symbol of their status, such as a double-pedestal desk, their feelings of personal integrity would not be greatly violated. But, how true is this of other persons and groups whose social places in the organization are not so secure? Our observer has this question in mind as he goes on to observe and interview the foremen and the workers.

[9] In fairness to our observer, it may be well here to defend him against a possible misunderstanding. In looking for objects which tend to differentiate groups from one another, he is no carping critic. He is not making any moral judgment, and he is not saying anything about whether there is fair or unfair discrimination between groups. These are sentiments which members of the organization may express on occasions, but the observer sees to it that his own sentiments are not acted upon. He is merely observing facts of social organization. Let us remember that he has probably never heard anything about the "classless society," and that if he has heard about it he has, no doubt, labeled it a myth or fiction.

THE OBSERVER LOOKS AT A SHOP DEPARTMENT AND INTERVIEWS SOME WORKERS

While walking through the shops, our observer has a number of interesting experiences. One experience in particular impresses him. One day he enters a shop department unobserved. There is a buzz of conversation, and the men seem to be working at great speed. Suddenly there is a sharp hissing sound. The conversation dies away, and there is a noticeable slowing up in the work pace. Later he discovers from a man in this shop whom he interviews that he had been mistaken for a rate setter. One of the workers, who acted as a lookout, had stepped on a valve releasing compressed air, which was a prearranged signal among the men for slowing down.

From this and similar experiences, the observer becomes aware of the protective attitudes which surround a shop department. Any person unknown to the workers who expresses more than a casual interest in their work or affairs is likely to be regarded with suspicion unless he takes pains to state clearly to them just what he is doing and why. Even then, they may not believe him and may alter their work habits and behavior in defense. These attitudes of suspicion, the observer notes, have a parallel in the suspicion toward the stranger manifested by many closely knit societies.

Attitudes of resistance to change, particularly to any change which might possibly affect their routine relations to one another, are so strong among certain employee groups that sometimes they are manifested in rather peculiar ways. In certain piecework groups, for example, the observer finds that social pressure by the employees themselves is directed against the fast worker. Workers who produce more than what the group considers a fair day's work are looked upon with disfavor by their fellow workers. They are subjected to sarcasm and ridicule and are called names, such as "speed king," "slave," and "rate buster." Inasmuch as the observer understands that under the group piecework system the more each worker produces, the more he earns, this behavior impresses him as being quite extraordinary. The expert on wage incentive systems had pointed out to him that this system had been designed for the workers' economic advantage. If this is so, the workers must be acting contrary to their own pecuniary interests. The observer decides to investigate further, and he interviews some of the workers who manifest this behavior.

The observer is impressed with the lack of comprehension some of the workers have of the way in which their earnings are computed. One worker tells him, for example, that his hours of work have been reduced by forty-five minutes per day. His supervisor told the men in his group that if they turned out as much work in the shorter time as they had before, their earnings would not be affected. He and his fellow workers agreed to try, and they were greatly surprised to find that their earnings did remain the same.

Other workers are more articulate. They explain to him that the reasons they behave the way they do are: (1) to prevent their piece rates from being cut; (2) to prevent their rates of performance from being raised or speeded up; and (3) to protect their fellow workers who may work more slowly from being bawled out or discharged by the foreman.[10]

The observer is interested in these reasons, particularly from this point of view: How effective is the practice of restriction of output in achieving the ends the employees seek and in controlling some of those things they fear may happen? Here is the curious situation he finds: Changes in piece rates, in hours of work, and in number of people employed are often related to factors completely outside the control of the worker, and sometimes even of management. Changes in piece rates occur

[10] See Stanley B. Mathewson, *Restriction of Output among Unorganized Workers* (New York: The Viking Press, 1931).

most frequently where there is a change in manufacturing process, and changes in manufacturing process are made by engineers whose chief function it is to reduce unit cost wherever the saving will justify the change. In some instances, changes occur irrespective of direct labor cost. Moreover, where labor is a substantial element, restriction of output tends to increase unit costs and instead of warding off a change in the piece rate may actually induce one.

Our observer concludes that the belief which these workers entertain in regard to this practice, that they can control the actions of management by behaving in a certain way, is very similar to the belief of certain primitive peoples that they can control a flood by performing certain rituals. It is his opinion that the workers' beliefs, and the actions with which they are associated, are in a relation of mutual dependence with certain very powerful sentiments, and that these sentiments are related to the workers' position in the social organization of the company.[11]

In this connection, one interview interests the observer particularly. The employee is complaining about his wages. As the observer listens to this man express his grievance, he gradually begins to understand what the locus of the complaint is. The employee is complaining because a certain worker in his department is earning more money than he is, and he does not see why this should be so. His supervisor has told him that this other fellow's job has a higher base rate than his job has. But still he does not see why there should be a difference. From the point of view of his own feelings and sentiments, as

[11] This statement implies nothing about the workers' being more "irrational" or "nonlogical" than any other group in industry. By acting in accordance with the codes of behavior considered appropriate to their group, they are being "social" and are not acting any differently from any well-integrated members of a closely knit group. Sometimes the codes of certain employee groups are at variance with the technical and economic objectives of the company as a whole.

well as those of many of his fellow workers, the job he is doing is considered more important and demands as much, if not more, skill and experience than the other job. The worker is indignant over the injustice of the matter. He feels he is being treated unfairly.

Our observer decides to interview the specialist who has charge of grading the different jobs in terms of the skill and responsibility required. This expert tells him how all the jobs in the factory have been carefully analyzed in terms of certain "objective" criteria and how in terms of these criteria they have been arranged in an ascending scale of labor grades. The lowest grade covers the simplest types of operations; the highest grade covers the operations involving the greatest amount of skill or responsibility; all other operations are placed in intermediate grades according to the skill or responsibility involved. Ranges of pay are established for these labor grades.

"But what do you do if the evaluations of 'job difficulty' you arrive at by 'objective' investigation do not agree with the evaluations the workers themselves make of these jobs?" asks our observer. The expert answers that he is not concerned with these "subjective" evaluations. The observer begins to wonder how often systems and plans for promoting efficiency in the organization fail to take into account the sentiments and feelings of the people who work under them. If this is a general practice, here is a clue to the real reasons for the workers' attitude of resistance to change which he has noted.

CONCLUSIONS

The tour is now over. Our observer has talked to an economist, and he has spent many days in a large industrial plant observing and interviewing people at work, from those at the top of the organization to those at the very bottom. He has pointed out certain facts of social organization that he has noticed. Let us now see if we can restate some of the things he has called to our attention.

(1) An industrial organization is composed of a number of people with characteristics and relationships which vary from person to person. Many different persons — bosses, technical specialists, supervisors, factory workers, elevator operators, and scrubwomen — are interacting daily with one another, and from their associations certain relationships are formed among them. Some of these relationships fall into routine patterns, such as the relationship between superior and subordinate, or between office workers and shop workers. These routine patterns of relationship and behavior, together with the objects that symbolize them, constitute the social organization of an industrial enterprise. Both the kind of behavior that is expected of a person and the kind of behavior he can expect from others are prescribed by these patterns. Most members of an industrial organization accept them as obvious and act as they dictate.

(2) From this point of view, the behavior of no one person in an industrial organization, from the very top to the very bottom, can be regarded as motivated by strictly economic or logical considerations. Routine patterns of interaction involve strong sentiments. Each group in the organization manifests its own powerful sentiments. It is likely that much of the behavior of many staff specialists which goes under the name of "efficiency" is as much the manifestation of a very strong sentiment — the sentiment or desire to originate new combinations — as it is of anything strictly logical.

(3) The meanings which any person in an industrial organization assigns to the events and objects in his environment are often determined by the patterns of interaction in which the events and objects occur. The significance to an employee of a double-pedestal desk, of a particular kind of pencil, or of a handset telephone is determined by the social setting in which

these objects appear. If people with double-pedestal desks originate action on people with single-pedestal desks, then double-pedestal desks become symbols of status or prestige in the organization. As patterns of behavior become crystallized, every object in the environment tends to take on a fixed social significance. It becomes easy to tell a person's social place in the organization by the objects which he wears and carries and which surround him. In these terms it can be seen how the introduction of a technical change may also involve for an individual or group of individuals the loss of certain prestige symbols and, as a result, have a demoralizing effect.

(4) It is neither convenient nor advisable to consider the behavior of any one group in an industrial organization as something apart from the relations which this group has with other groups in the organization. Behavior at the work level, for example, cannot be considered as something apart from and unrelated to the behavior of top management, the behavior of staff specialists, or the behavior of supervisors. Manifestations of resistance to change at the work level offer a good example, for they are closely related to the social position of the workers, who are at the bottom level of a highly stratified organization. In terms of interaction, the workers are in a position of having action originated upon them more often than upon any other group. They are constantly having to accommodate themselves to changes which they do not initiate. Their position is sometimes comparable to the position of businessmen in the 1930's in relation to the political administration. They also want a breathing spell.

(5) Although the workers may not be organized in the sense of belonging to a union, they are organized in the sense that they participate in those patterns of interrelations which go to make up the social organization of the company. Indeed, the employees of an industrial concern are far from being the undifferentiated group the organization chart suggests. They

are related to one another by the technological processes they serve, and each occupational group has its own way of living, its own codes of behavior, its own powerful sentiments, and its own rank in the social scale. At times these groups may be very important factors in the total social organization, especially if they are ignored or if the functions they fulfill for their members are not sufficiently appreciated.

(6) If communication and collaboration between groups in industry are to be effective, it is as important, if not more important, for top management to understand and appreciate the behavior of the people at the bottom level as it is for the bottom group to understand the logical and economic objectives of the top. At present, there seems to be no group in industry whose responsibility it is to see that those people who are responsible for originating action are provided with an accurate picture of behavior at the work level. It is important that those abstractions, such as efficiency, costs, etc., in terms of which the activities of industry are carried on do not entirely exclude the factor of human interaction.

CHAPTER VI

OF WORDS AND MEN

THE thesis of this chapter will consist of two points: (1) a good portion of the executive's environment is verbal, far more than he sometimes seems to realize; (2) little attention has been explicitly given, either by the executive or by students of administration, to the skills required in handling the verbal environment. The executive often has no conceptual framework in terms of which he can deal with it, nothing comparable at least to the explicit skills with which he handles his external nonhuman environment.

THE EXECUTIVE'S ENVIRONMENT IS VERBAL

That a good portion of the executive's environment is verbal seems hardly open to question. In discussions, meetings, and conferences the verbal atmosphere is thick. The executive is dealing largely with words, symbols, and abstractions. Of course, this applies to any one of us. We are all responding to words and other stimuli involving meaning. It seems to me obvious, however, that the higher the executive goes in an organization the more important it becomes for him, if he is to handle effectively one aspect of his job, to deal competently with his verbal environment.

On the one hand, he has to become skillful in using words that will appeal to his listeners' sentiments. In trying to secure the coöperation of individuals in the common purposes of the enterprise the executive often has to practice the art of persuasion. He uses words that he hopes will produce the appropriate effects on his listeners. In statements to stockholders, employees, and customers, the executive has to resort to words, both oral and written. In handling complaints and grievances, the executive is using, as well as listening to, words.

On the other hand, the executive has to be able to interpret skillfully what people say, for in so far as his work involves the interactions of human beings his data come from what he hears as well as from what he sees and does.[1] Whether he likes it or not, he has to practice this difficult art; yet he has no explicit tools for doing it. He either picks up the skill intuitively or tries to organize his work so that the need for exercising it is at a minimum. This latter method is likely to be unsuccessful because it leads him to busy himself more and more with logical, statistical, and oversimplified abstractions or lofty principles about human motivation and conduct. In doing so he loses touch with the concrete situation before him.

In short, words play an important role in all the major functions of the executive. If this proposition is true, it seems sensible to ask what the executive needs to know about words and their functions and what skills he can explicitly develop in interpreting what people say.

THE FUNCTIONS OF LANGUAGE OR WORDS

Let us consider some of the different functions of language or words.[2] In the first place, words can be used to refer to events and happenings outside of our skin: this can be called the logico-experimental function of language. In this way words are used by scientists or by two or more people engaged in a discussion of matters with which they have firsthand, familiar, and intuitive acquaintance, as well as a common back-

[1] These statements are similar to those made about the social scientist by Professor L. J. Henderson in *Three Lectures on Concrete Sociology* (privately distributed), p. 13.

[2] For the purposes of this paper it would be inappropriate to discuss the many different theories of language. Only three well-recognized functions of language will be mentioned to illustrate some of the problems involved in interpreting what people say.

ground of systematic knowledge. The words and symbols used by the speaker refer to events, and uniformities among events, which occur primarily outside of him or the listener, and to which they can go for observation and check in case of disagreement. Most of us spend only a very small portion of our day using words in this strict sense. We are much more likely to be engaged in less arduous and more pleasant verbal practices.

In a social conversation, for example, the situation is likely to be quite different. When two or more people are talking together, what is primarily happening is an interaction of sentiments rather than anything strictly logical. One person is using words to express certain sentiments, to which the other responds with similar or opposing sentiments; or one person tries to influence the other by using symbols that will have a favorable reaction on the latter's sentiments. This can be called the "emotive"[3] function of language, as opposed to the logico-experimental. The skillful politician is a good example of a person using words in this way.

There is a third function of language which has received considerable attention during the past two or three decades. Through words man not only communicates but satisfies his desires. I refer to the day-dreaming, revery, and air-castle building in which we all indulge and from which we obtain considerable satisfaction. A good portion of our day is spent in using words to satisfy our desires in this way.

That "Language serves a man not only to express something but also to express himself,"[4] every executive should realize and explicitly take into account. The fact that language has different functions and that these functions, except under special

[3] Taken from C. K. Ogden and I. A. Richards, *The Meaning of Meaning* (New York: Harcourt, Brace and Company, 1925), p. 257.

[4] *Ibid.*, p. 261 (statement by G. von der Gabelentz, quoted by Ogden and Richards).

circumstances, are rarely distinguished complicates our problem. Words refer not only to things happening outside our skins, but also to our attitudes, feelings, and sentiments toward these objects and events. This means that many statements are expressed which have little or no meaning apart from the personal situation of the person who makes them. This not only makes the interpretation of what people say difficult, it also makes it imperative to do a skillful job, because if we refer words to a wrong context we are likely to misunderstand what a person is telling us. The channels of communication in a business organization often become clogged because words are referred to wrong contexts.

The problem would be simple if when people spoke they labeled what it was they were telling us; if, for example, they would say: "Now I am talking about simple events and uniformities among them in our common experience." "Now I am expressing my sentiments and attitude toward something." "Now I am day-dreaming and satisfying my ego." "Now I am trying to disguise my sentiments as logic." "Now I am trying to influence your sentiments by using these particular words." "Now you may think I am talking about my supervisor but really I am talking about my unhappy experiences with my father." Unfortunately (or fortunately, depending upon our point of view), this is not often true. We very seldom express our sentiments *as sentiments*. One of the most time-consuming pastimes of the human mind is to rationalize sentiments and to disguise sentiments as logic.

THE SKILL OF INTERPRETING WHAT PEOPLE SAY

All I have said so far shows clearly that the interpretation of what people say is a difficult business. There is nothing to be gained by pretending that the job is simple. It is something that some people learn from experience and at which some people — physicians, lawyers, and businessmen — become exceedingly skillful. (These skillful people, however, often cannot communicate their skill.) The technique cannot be learned without practice but, again, for some people practice is not enough. No matter how much experience they have in listening to or in using words, they never acquire any great ability in this field. They continue to deal with words as constants rather than as variables, as if they had universal meanings rather than different meanings for different people under different conditions and situations. Some academic people are the worst offenders in this respect. Some scientists and engineers can never learn that words outside of the limited area of their specialty have different uses and important social functions.

Dr. Henderson has said: "Effective rules of procedure in interpreting what men say have not yet been developed . . . Therefore we are in respect of this kind of work still more or less in the master-apprentice stage."[5] However, in the past twelve years the research group with which I am associated has had considerable experience in trying to interpret what people say. It may be of some interest, therefore, if I try to state more explicitly some of the rules or discriminations which we have worked out. It may seem rather absurd to try to communicate a skill which, like any other, is in certain respects ineffable. However, inasmuch as all of us are practicing it, some more successfully than others, it can do no harm and perhaps some good to try to state more explicitly its nature. What I shall say, of course, can be only very rough, approximate, and tentative.

Getting People to Talk about Matters Important to Them

When I am confronted with a complex situation involving the interactions of people, what people say is necessarily an important part of the data from which I have to make a diagnosis. Therefore, my first object is to get people to talk freely and

[5] Henderson, *Three Lectures on Concrete Sociology*, p. 19.

frankly about matters which are important to them. This situation in which I try to get people to talk I shall call the interview. In the interview I use a number of simple rules or ideas: I listen. I do not interrupt. I do not give advice. I avoid leading questions. I refrain from making moral judgments about the opinions expressed. I do not express my own opinions, beliefs, or sentiments. I avoid argument at all cost. I do this by seeing to it that the speaker's sentiments do not react on my own. Inasmuch as these rules have been stated elsewhere, I shall not elaborate on them here.[6]

Orientation to Speaker

Although it is sometimes difficult to get people to talk freely about matters of importance to them, it is not nearly so difficult as the next part of my job. While I am listening intently and sympathetically to what the person is saying, my mind is not just a blank. I am listening for something; there is some framework in which my thought is set. I am oriented to the speaker in a certain way. To take an example, let us assume that an employee in a large factory is speaking to me: he says, "The supervisors in this company are a bunch of goddam slavedrivers." What is my attitude toward such a remark?

First, I am not interested in the verbal definition of the word "slavedriver." Secondly, I do not allow my sentiments to be acted upon by this word, nor do I try to argue the speaker out of his belief. Thirdly, I am not assuming that there exists one particular quality in some supervisors to which this word

[6] These rules for interviewing are described more fully in the following publications: L. J. Henderson, "Physician and Patient as a Social System," *The New England Journal of Medicine*, vol. 212, no. 18, May, 1935, pp. 819–823; Elton Mayo, *The Human Problems of an Industrial Civilization* (New York: Macmillan, 1933), pp. 91–92; F. J. Roethlisberger and W. J. Dickson, *Management and the Worker* (Cambridge: Harvard University Press, 1939), pp. 270–291.

refers; that is, I do not assume that because there is a word "slavedriver" there is only one thing to which it refers. Finally, I am not assuming that truth or falsity has anything to do with the statement.[7]

How, then, am I oriented to such a remark? In the first place, I assume that this person is expressing his feelings and sentiments. I assume that these feelings and sentiments are not "words," although words are being used to express them. I assume that I shall not be able to understand the feelings and sentiments expressed until I find the context to which they refer. In order to find the context, I am thinking of those events in the life of the employee to which his statement may refer, and also of the social situations in which they occurred. In other words, I am hunting for the referents of the statement. Therefore, I try to get the employee to talk about the particular supervisors (Supervisor 1, Supervisor 2, etc.) with whom he has been associated — when, where, how often, under what conditions, and so on. I am listening for what these particular supervisors did and under what conditions they did it, what meanings the employee assigned to their behavior, what the employee did and under what conditions he did it, and so on.

But more than this, I am also thinking of, and trying to get the employee to talk about, events in his previous history or in his associations with people outside the factory to which events involving interactions with people within the factory may be related *for the employee*. I do this because I assume that this particular employee's unpleasant feelings about a particular supervisor are a resultant of two sets of factors: (1) what he (the employee) is bringing to the situation in terms of hopes and expectations (sentiments), and (2) the social demands which the situation is making of him.

[7] Perhaps I should say, "I try not to let myself take these customary attitudes toward words," but this is often easier said than done.

(1) In order to find out what the employee is bringing to the situation in terms of sentiments, I need to know something about the meaningful associations he has had with other people and groups before coming to the factory. I assume that from these previous associations he has been conditioned to a certain way of life and to certain hopes, fears, and expectations. In terms of this kind of data, I can see more clearly what sentiments of the employee are being violated, disregarded, or misunderstood by a particular supervisor. I may find, for example, that the employee's attitude toward supervision is rooted somewhere in his attitude toward authority as conditioned by his early family situation; on anyone in authority he may be projecting the parental image.

(2) But if I stopped here I might still be missing an important context to which his statement may refer. This worker is not an isolated individual. He has relations with other people. He is part of a social system called the factory. He is part of a smaller social system called the department. He is part of a still smaller social system called the work group — those people with whom he is associating daily at work. It may be that in the small work group this employee is an informal leader. The workers respect him as a craftsman; they go to him for help about their work; they go to him with their troubles. He instructs them about difficult jobs and he listens to their grievances. Perhaps the foreman of his department does not recognize this employee's status in the informal work situation or, if he does, has not seen to it that his superiors also recognize it. Perhaps through ignorance of the situation he has recently promoted a younger and shorter-service man to a supervisory job in this department, a man whose efficiency record is good, and who is therefore easier to recommend to his superiors for promotion, but who is looked upon by his own work associates as a "rate buster," "chiseler," or "squealer." Perhaps it is the disturbances within this social situation to which the employee's

statement, "The supervisors in this company are a bunch of goddam slavedrivers," refers.

I need not emphasize that it is important to know what a person is really complaining about before trying to act on the verbal manifestation of his complaint. Otherwise, we shall be dealing only with words, or symptoms, rather than with the situation determining the grievance.

So far, I have told you of my attitude in an interview toward a person when he is complaining about another person, but my attitude is very similar if he is complaining about nonhuman objects and events in his experience. (I say "in an interview" because this is not my ordinary social attitude.) If a person tells me, for example, that his desk is too small, I do not try to convince him that the size of his desk is sufficient for his purposes; I am thinking of the social setting in which desks appear in his work situation. What human relationship does the desk symbolize for him? It may be that in his organization the higher in the business structure the person goes, the bigger the desk becomes. It may be that the person who is talking to me is a college man with a burning desire to succeed. He may be indulging in a little wishful thinking; by getting a bigger desk he may think he is elevating himself in the company. When he complains that his desk is too small, he may really be telling me about his dissatisfaction with his advancement in the company. If so, I get him to talk about that.

DIAGNOSING HUMAN SITUATIONS

In discussing how I interpret what people say, I have also been describing how I go about diagnosing a personal situation, that is, how I go from what people say to what their situation is. Obviously, it is the situation to which the words refer that is important and not the words themselves. *It is the situation and not the words that we want to understand.* I assume here that just as control of our physical environment came when we were able to control the objects and events to which words refer, so human control begins when we can control the human situations to which words refer.

In diagnosing human situations I try to avoid two tricks which words can play: (1) The danger of treating alike by words things that are different and unique, and (2) the danger of separating by words things that are inseparable in fact.[8]

Treating Alike by Words Situations that are Different

In our ordinary language we often use one word to refer to many unique objects in many different settings and in many different stages of process. For example, we have one word "chair" to refer to many unique objects, such as Chair 1, Chair 2, Chair 3, etc. We have one word "chair" to refer to Chair 1, which Smith 1 (the boss) occupies, and Chair 2, which Smith 2 (the secretary) occupies. The behavior of people toward the person who occupies Chair 1 is quite different from their behavior toward the person using Chair 2. The duties, obligations, and privileges of the occupant of Chair 1 are quite different from those of the occupant of Chair 2. Very seldom, at least in large business organizations, does Smith 1 sit on Chair 2. Even less often does Smith 2 sit on Chair 1, at least if Smith 1 is present; it would be considered inappropriate behavior if she did, if not by Smith 1 then by Smith 3 (Smith 1's boss). Moreover, we have the same word "chair" to refer to Chair 3 when it was in the boss's office ten years ago and Chair 3 when it has become old and dilapidated and is being used by the janitor in the basement.

Thus, our ordinary language tends to make the objects and events in our experience appear in isolation, that is, apart from their context. This is particularly true of common objects, such as chairs and desks, which occur in events involving human

[8] For the ideas expressed in this section I am greatly indebted to A. Korzybski, *Science and Sanity* (New York: The Science Press Printing Co., 1933).

interactions. They appear in a certain time setting, that is, they are preceded by certain events and followed by others; moreover, they appear in a certain social setting. Therefore, if we pay exclusive attention to words and exclude the situations to which the words refer we miss very important differences of context. We fall into the error of assuming that because the same word can be applied to many different objects and events in different situations they are in some way the same. As a result, we fail to notice differences, and we read into our experience similarities where differences exist. Therefore, whenever I am concerned with overt or verbal behavior involving the interactions of human beings I am alert to differences in situation and I look for differences before I look for uniformities.

Let me give an example of what I mean. Let us assume that we have been called in to study a large company which has had in operation for a number of years a bonus plan for its executives; the management is interested to know whether or not the bonus is acting as an incentive. How do we approach such a problem? Can we assume that because there is one word "executive" all the persons to whom this label applies are the same and the "bonus" means the same thing to each of them? Can we assume that because there is one word "incentive" there is one thing to which this word applies? Can we determine the effects of the bonus on something before we diagnose what that something is? Or do we look first at the particular people, the particular interrelations among them, and the particular situations in which the words "executive," "incentive," and "bonus" appear?

If we follow this last procedure, what do we find? We find Executive 1 with a particular background and social conditioning (private hopes, fears, sentiments, which we shall refer to as SC_1) in association with people in a particular department (Department 1) and a particular division (Division 1), i.e., a member of a particular social system (codes, customs, and social routines of behavior, which we shall refer to as SS_1). Schematically the situation can be represented as follows:[9]

$$SC_1 \longleftrightarrow E_1 \longleftrightarrow SS_1$$

This is a shorthand way of representing a particular executive's situation as "a system of equilibrium" resulting from (1) certain demands which he is bringing to the situation as a result of his particular past personal history, and (2) certain social demands which are being made of him as a member of a particular social system. The situation of Executive 2 in Department 2 and Division 2 would look like this:

$$SC_2 \longleftrightarrow E_2 \longleftrightarrow SS_2$$

After studying the executives in the company from this point of view, let us ask what effects the bonus might be expected to have. Schematically again, we may represent the situation for four different executives in four different divisions of the company as follows:

Bonus

$\updownarrow$

$$SC_1 \longleftrightarrow E_1 \longleftrightarrow SS_1 \longleftrightarrow \text{Effects}_{1,\,2,\,3,}\ \text{etc.}$$
$$SC_2 \longleftrightarrow E_2 \longleftrightarrow SS_2 \longleftrightarrow \text{Effects}_{4,\,5,\,6,}\ \text{etc.}$$
$$SC_3 \longleftrightarrow E_3 \longleftrightarrow SS_3 \longleftrightarrow \text{Effects}_{7,\,8,\,9,}\ \text{etc.}$$
$$SC_4 \longleftrightarrow E_4 \longleftrightarrow SS_4 \longleftrightarrow \text{Effects}_{10,\,11,\,12,}\ \text{etc.}$$

Looking at the problem from this point of view, we might expect to find, first, that there are as many different effects from the bonus as there are different executives or different kinds of executive situations. Secondly, we might find that there are as

[9] This is, of course, an oversimplified representation. The executive is a member of more than one social system. However, for the present purposes of illustration, this representation of the executive's situation is sufficient.

many different effects from the bonus as there are different social systems. We might find that a bonus plan is in fact a different system as applied to different social organizations. Only after we have broken down our data into these differences, however, do we look for uniformities. Only in this way can we avoid reading verbal similarities into things that are different.

With this kind of approach, what happens to our original question of whether or not the bonus acts as an incentive? Like many questions that the human mind can devise, it becomes meaningless, and like many meaningless questions, such as "How many angels can sit on the point of a needle?" it has no meaningful answer. Some of us find it difficult to throw a question overboard. We feel that *because we can frame a simple question there must be a simple answer*, and to give up such a question is like parting with our best friend or our favorite hat. To those who can free themselves from sentimental attachments to words, however, it becomes apparent that by giving up the question nothing is lost — at least, nothing is lost from the point of view of knowledge; indeed, there is something gained. We know in fact some of the effects the bonus is now having on particular persons in particular positions in a particular organization. In these terms new questions can be raised by means of which we may learn more; and from this new knowledge the bonus plan may be better evaluated.

Separating by Words Things that are Inseparable in Fact

In diagnosing human situations there is also the danger of separating by words things that are inseparable in fact. It is important, in tracing expressions of sentiment to the events in a person's experience to which they refer, to keep the events in their context; in other words, it is important to keep together those things which are together when experienced.

For example, from the above diagram it can be seen that the

executive is kept together with the social system to which he is contributing his services, and together with his social conditioning. These things are kept together because they are together in his experience. An executive apart from a personal history would be something no one has seen anywhere, any time. An executive apart from a coöperative system ceases to be an executive. He may be an executive out of a job; but this is a different context from that of our illustration.

THREE DIFFERENT PERSONAL SITUATIONS

So far, we have considered how to get a person to talk freely about things that are important to him and how the listener is oriented to the speaker in order to interpret skillfully what he says. We have seen some of the ways in which words can prevent us from understanding a concrete situation. We have seen the necessity of looking for differences in our data before searching for simple uniformities. Although each human situation is unique, there are certain uniformities which begin to emerge after a large number of people have been interviewed. There are three uniformities which I have found among a number of persons I have interviewed and in terms of which I make my first rough diagnosis. As I listen to a person in the manner I have described, I am roughly asking three questions and I am roughly expecting three answers:

(1) Am I listening to a person who is well related to the work group of which he is a member; and, therefore, am I listening essentially to the sentiments of the social system to which he belongs — the routines of collaboration of his group — the norms and codes of behavior of his group — the organizational way of thinking and the customary way of doing things? Or am I listening to a person who in practically everything he says is expressing a lack of relationship, or a defective relationship, to his work group? In the latter

case,

(2) Am I listening to the "obsessive thinking" of a person who, outside of the family, has never achieved in all his experience an effective or intimate relationship with his contemporaries or with his own age group, or

(3) Am I listening to a person whose disequilibrium, or lack of orientation to his social surrounding, is not so much due to his early social conditioning as to his inability to adjust readily and without assistance to changes in his present environment? Is this a man who has lost his way because his customary and routine relations with people were altered too rapidly by demotion, promotion, transference, or some technical change in his work?

People in these three quite different human situations will respond to the systems, policies, and practices about them in three quite different ways. In any business organization (if there is not a strike in process) there will probably be a large proportion of Class 1. Wherever there is a great deal of discontent, one can probably find a number of the Class 3 group. In any large concern, however, no matter how well run, there are likely to be Class 3 situations which need attention, although some of them recover their equilibrium without any help. Class 2 people will probably not stay very long in a business organization without considerable attention being given them; they are likely to be found among the newcomers.

THE EXECUTIVE NOT ONLY LISTENS; HE ALSO USES WORDS

We have considered the executive as a listener who is trying to interpret skillfully what people say in order that he may be better able to understand and control the human situations about him. But the executive not only listens; he speaks and uses words in written and oral statements to other members of the organization. As a result, other people in the organization are in a position of understanding or misunderstanding, correctly interpreting or misinterpreting, what he says. This raises a number of problems concerning the communication of matters that are related to the feelings and sentiments of people. Executives are not always communicating strictly logical propositions.

With the use of language for the purpose of transmitting factual information we shall not be concerned; although errors may arise, they are the kind of errors which sooner or later can be corrected. But matters are not so simple when language is used to influence behavior by appealing to feelings and sentiments. In this area misunderstandings multiply rapidly, and they are difficult to correct.

It is not our purpose here to consider the different techniques of verbal persuasion that have been developed in advertising and mediums of propaganda. We shall consider the use of words for persuasion only in relation to the administrative context, and in terms of this context we shall make only a few observations.

It is interesting to note that in business today, particularly in manufacturing organizations, it is not considered quite appropriate for the executive to indulge in statements of sentiment when talking to his employees and fellow associates. This form of behavior is the province of his salesforce when appealing to a particular customer, or when talking to the public on the air, or through other mediums of advertising. With regard to employer-employee relations, however, the executive code dictates that employers should interact with their employees merely on the basis of fact. This code has led to a curious state of affairs. It has blinded some executives to what is going on around them. It has forced some into a position of trying to handle matters of sentiment as if they were matters of fact. And when matters of sentiment so blatantly arise that even the most obtuse cannot fail to label them for what they are, they have no techniques for dealing with them.

Skills Involved in Handling Matters of Sentiment

This latter case was forcibly brought to my attention the other day by the captain of a ship in the merchant marine. He had gone to sea as a boy and had been brought up in the tradition that the captain is master of the ship: his word at sea is law. Although he was kindly toward his crew, all his reflexes had been conditioned to this tradition. As a result, for years he failed to see that his authority depended only upon the fact that his junior officers and crew also accepted and upheld the tradition. And then things at sea began to change. People who had not been so well conditioned for coöperation, and particularly for coöperation on the basis of this tradition, began to join his crew. The code began to change. The captain had to meet with his crew and listen to some of their complaints and grievances. In one instance he was confronted with a long list of complaints about the food. One item on this list was to the effect that the crew did not get "seconds on jello." Now, it was at this point in the captain's story that his face became flushed and speech failed him. But his gestures of exasperation and frustration expressed only too well what he could not say in words. Imagine him — the captain — having to deal with people who made such ridiculous charges! Moreover, the actual fact was that they *could* get "seconds on jello." In the face of this problem, the captain was helpless. All his conditioned reflexes could do was to produce sputtering noises. He had no skills for handling this ridiculous situation. His sense of humor was gone; his ordinary social insight was gone. He could not remember the social mechanisms he had used when he was a boy to "get somebody's goat." In the face of this situation, the captain could only talk about "communism," "fifth-column activities," "agitators," "aliens," and then, as the story developed, get sick with a case of shingles.[10]

[10] It may be well to point out that the captain is a Class 3 situation as above

This is not intended as a funny story, nor to cast any aspersions on the captain. None of us would want to be in his position. He was up against a difficult human problem, even though it manifested itself at the level of "seconds on jello." The only point I want to make is to show the state of affairs into which we can get when we try to handle matters of sentiment as if they were matters of fact. For the captain, a difficult problem of human diagnosis was involved which entailed going from the symptoms to the underlying human situation among his crew. But for this he received no help; he had no skills, and his conditioned reflexes could only make matters worse both for himself and for the crew.

The Tendency to Deal with Employees on a Basis of Facts Alone

In the past several years, considerable emphasis has been placed upon providing information to employees about the economic conditions of the business. Many concerns have prepared interesting, attractive, graphic reports which would be intelligible to the layman. Underlying this tendency to communicate simple economic facts to employees has been the assumption that labor difficulties primarily arose because the employees were not sufficiently acquainted with the economic purposes and problems of the company. That there is some truth in this assumption may be granted; the interesting thing to note, however, is again the tendency to deal with employees on a basis of facts alone. It happens, however, that loyalty and confidence are matters of feeling and sentiment and are not necessarily secured by this approach, as any skillful politician knows.

In collective bargaining activities the same tendency prevails in many organizations. Elaborate charts and diagrams are prepared to show that the charges or demands made by the union

described. His customary ways of dealing with people were no longer adequate in the new situation in which he found himself.

are not accurate or reasonable in terms of the facts, sometimes even to show that in fact they are served "seconds on jello." In the battle to decide who is right and who is wrong, human situations involving simple matters of sentiment are ignored.

THE EXERCISE OF HUMAN CONTROL BY LISTENING BEFORE TALKING

That the executive in dealing with human beings should take on some of the behavior patterns of the politician is not being suggested by these observations. Nor is it being recommended that the executive should make Fourth of July speeches, although in this connection it is interesting to note the bifurcation in our modern industrial society: on the one hand, the industrial leader is supposed to secure the loyalty of his employees by appealing to facts, while, on the other hand, the political leader is allowed to secure the loyalty of his constituents by appealing to emotion. What is being suggested is more simple and is of this order:

(1) There are many words used by executives that not only communicate information, they convey sentiments.

(2) The persons to whom the words are addressed also have sentiments; their sentiments vary with age, sex, personal situation, official rank and informal position in the organization.

(3) Because these sentiments in part relate to the different positions which people occupy in the organization, then it follows that some words which are very meaningful to some members, or some parts of the organization, may have little or no meaning or different meanings to other members and other parts of the organization.

(4) This problem demands serious consideration. It is the problem of the effect on different members and on different parts of an organization of words used by the executive when he gives an instruction or order, when he

announces a policy, or when he prepares a statement addressed to employees or to stockholders. This point is very simple. The legal jargon of a lawyer may give aesthetic satisfaction to him and his fellow brethren, but it may send shivers down the spine of the layman. The exact and precise jargon of the engineer may not be communicating "facts" to the employees who are being addressed; it may be transmitting feelings of apprehension. Sometimes also, symbols may lose their customary and traditional significance, as our example of the captain in relation to his crew well illustrated. For seamen who demand "seconds on jello" symbols evoking the traditions of the sea have lost their power to motivate.

(5) Therefore, when talking to an individual or group, it is important to address oneself to their sentiments, so that on the one hand what one says will not be misunderstood, and on the other hand it will have the effect on the listeners that the speaker intends. But how does one address oneself to the listeners' sentiments? How does one know what they are? Here is where the "skill of listening" previously described comes in. This skill allows one to go from the words to the sentiments being expressed; but still more important, it allows one to go from the sentiments being expressed to the human situations underlying them. Words addressed to concrete human situations are likely to be more appropriate.

(6) Therefore, it is important for the executive *to listen* before talking. By this means he comes to understand the sentiments and situations of the person or group before he practices the art of persuasion or assurance in order to secure their loyalty, confidence, and coöperation. In any large-scale organization, where many layers of supervision separate the top from the bottom, these dual skills are needed. Only when the people at the top of the organization understand better the feelings and sentiments of the people at the bottom can

they communicate to the bottom what to top management is important, in a manner which will obtain the understanding and acceptance of those at the bottom. This is the exercise of human control by "understanding" and not by "verbal magic."

CHAPTER VII

WHAT IS ADEQUATE PERSONNEL MANAGEMENT?

MANY plans and systems of personnel management seem to me to be adequate in general but inadequate in particular. They address themselves to human nature in general but not to human beings in particular. They tend to be concerned with somebody and anybody, but with nobody in particular. My plea, therefore, will be for a personnel program that addresses itself to the concrete human situations in a particular plant.

It may be well to say at the outset that my comments will be primarily addressed to modern business organizations employing thousands of people and located in urban centers, organizations in which scientific management has been applied and which have undergone some standardization and specialization. The question, therefore, will be: What is adequate personnel management for such organizations?

To start answering this question requires that we first consider the major human problems which such an organization faces. With this clearly in mind we can then proceed in an orderly fashion to consider: Who in the organization is taking care of these problems? Are there any skills associated with the handling of these problems and, if so, what are they? How can they be applied? The answers to these questions will allow us then to restate our original question and suggest certain steps toward its solution.

THREE MAJOR HUMAN PROBLEMS IN A BUSINESS ORGANIZATION

The human problems of a business organization can be conceived of in a number of different ways. Customarily we think of them in terms of the development of personnel functions. (1) There are problems of employment and placement: how to select the right people and how to place them in the right jobs. (2) There are problems of training: how to instruct new workers in the techniques of their job and in their responsibilities. (3) There are problems relating to working conditions, safety, and health: how to maintain reasonable hours of work and congenial and healthful conditions of work, and how to prevent accidents and lost time due to illness. (4) There are problems relating to payment: how to pay workers adequately for the work they do. (5) There are problems relating to promotion: how to advance people in accordance with their abilities. (6) There are problems relating to the welfare of employees: how to help them in times of need and at retirement, as well as to provide recreational and social activities during their period of employment. (7) There are problems of collective bargaining: how to give employees the opportunity of saying and doing something with regard to the conditions of their employment.

There is no question that this system of classifying human problems is useful and practical for certain purposes. However, inasmuch as a great deal has already been said in terms of these functions, it might be interesting to restate the human problems of a business organization from a different point of view. The new way of classifying human problems which this point of view suggests does not supplant the former. It is merely another way of conceiving of the human problems of a business organization, which we hope to show is also useful, convenient, and practical for certain purposes.

According to this conception, the first human problem of any business organization is *how to secure the coöperation of people in attaining its collective purpose.* Every personnel function above described is in part related to this objective. However, many of these functions are so conceived of and so stated as to be directly associated with the more technical methods of securing efficiently the economic objective of the total organization. For our purposes, we feel it is important to keep separate these two aspects of coöperative activity. By keeping clear (1) the processes required to secure the economic purposes of the business organization from (2) the processes required to secure the coöperation of people in attaining these purposes, we avoid talking at the same time about what may be two quite different things.

If the first human problem is how to secure collaboration among members of the working force, then some of the subordinate problems relating to it can be roughly divided into three groups: (1) problems relating to the channels of communication within the organization through which employees can learn about their duties and obligations in relation to the economic purpose, as well as express their feelings and sentiments about their methods and conditions of work; (2) problems of maintaining a condition of balance within the internal organization such that employees, by contributing their services, are able to satisfy their desires and hence are willing to coöperate; and (3) problems of effecting individual adjustments, whereby particular employees who are having difficulties can be assisted to become better oriented to their situations.

Problems of Communication

How can the people at the top of the organization — that is, those who are responsible for making decisions and originating action — be kept in touch with what is happening at the work level? This seems to me to be one of the major human problems of large-scale industry, where there exists considerable separation, both spatial and social, between the top and the bottom of the organization. Under such conditions, it is difficult for top management to have the intimate, firsthand acquaintance with the working force that can be obtained in a smaller enterprise.

How can the bottom of the organization be kept informed with regard to the economic purposes of the people at the top? How can information be transmitted downward through the supervisory organization without distortion? This is also an important problem, although not quite so serious as the first, because more attention has been paid to it and because the nature of the relevant information going down is more easily communicable than the nature of the relevant information going up. Although this is not entirely true, as a first rough generalization it can be said that the communications going down are more likely to be concerned with tangible matters that can be seen and touched, whereas the communications going up are more likely to be concerned with more intangible matters—feelings and sentiments that can be heard but not directly seen.

Problems of Social Balance within the Organization

How can a plant be organized so as to fulfill its technical objective of manufacturing a product at a minimum cost and at the same time fulfill a social function of providing for its employees a socially significant way of life? How can a comfortable working equilibrium be maintained between the various social groups in an industrial enterprise such that no one group in the organization will separate itself out in opposition to the remainder? How can technical changes be introduced without disrupting too severely the social organization of the plant? How can people be transferred, promoted, upgraded, downgraded in a manner that will not impair the morale of the groups in which the movements of people occur? Here is another group of important human problems in modern industry.

Problems of Individual Work Effectiveness

How can employees be kept satisfactorily oriented to their jobs? This question implies more than job placement, as it is ordinarily understood. It means trying to understand the particular demands which an individual is making of his job and how his total situation is meeting or failing to meet these demands.

In modern industry more attention must be given to these problems of individual work effectiveness. Their solution requires an understanding of two complimentary processes. One is the process of trying to arrange the work situation so that the satisfactions from the job do not fall too far short of the demands that are being made of it. The other is the process of helping individual workers to modify the excessive and impossible demands which they may be making of the job. Many times these latter demands arise from experiences outside the work situation.

WHO IS TAKING CARE OF THESE PROBLEMS?

Adequate personnel management must, in some concrete way, face these three important human problems. They are not simple and easy problems to solve. They seem to be particularly acute in any large-scale modern corporation. Although any individual plant, no matter how large or how small, has these problems in some degree, their importance grows as the plant grows. The manager of a small plant does not need to give them his complete or sustained attention. His intimate and close association with the concrete situation makes it unnecessary for him to abstract them from the situation for special consideration. He can take them in his stride; handling them is part and parcel of his normal daily activities.

The manager of a large enterprise, however, cannot take them for granted. He cannot assume that the organization which he has set up for the fulfillment of certain economic objectives will provide him automatically with the information he needs about the human situations at the work level. Likewise, he can no longer assume that the necessary social conditions for collaboration are fulfilled by the work arrangements which his engineers and supervisors provide. He cannot assume that difficulties of adjustment of an individual employee to his job will be called to his attention, or to the attention of some other responsible person, at the time when it is exceedingly important for him or that person to know about them.

Who, then, is taking care of these problems in a business organization? In one sense, of course, it can be said that they are the direct responsibility of the executive and supervisory personnel, whose function it is to maintain a system of communication, as well as to secure the essential services from individuals.[1] But this does not quite answer the question we are raising: To what extent is explicit attention being given to these problems? To what extent can it be assumed that the formal system of communication provided for the fulfillment of the economic purpose can at the same time operate equally well in providing relevant information about human satisfactions and dissatisfactions at the work level? And what techniques and explicit skills for this latter purpose are used? Too often it is assumed that these human problems will take care of themselves or will be adequately taken care of by the intuitive insight of skillful executives, once the technical conditions of efficient production are maintained. As a result, there is no one group who is giving its complete, uninterrupted, and explicit attention to them.

It should also be noted that no matter how well each of the customary personnel functions previously mentioned is exercised, it cannot be assumed that these problems of communi-

[1] See Chester I. Barnard, *The Functions of the Executive* (Cambridge: Harvard University Press, 1938), Chapter XV, "The Executive Functions."

cation, of maintaining balance, and of effecting personal adjustments are being taken care of. The right person for a particular job may be selected, but he may become discontented if continuously or conspicuously mishandled. He may be well paid in relation to the standards of the community for such work, but his pay may not express his rightful position in the informal group of which he is a member and, as a result, it may be a source of irritation. His work may be surrounded with all the modern safeguards for his safety and health and yet fail to conform to his standards of conventional social living. He may be given an opportunity to express himself, but what he says may not be listened to or correctly interpreted. He may be given a ladder on which to climb, but this ladder may express certain values which have little or no meaning in his present situation. Opportunity may be knocking on his door, but there may be no one who can give him sufficient time and attention so that he can see it. For him there seems to be as little opportunity as in a graveyard or an old ladies' home — expressions which are commonly heard when interviewing workers.

It is apparent that if these problems are to be adequately dealt with there must be in a business organization some group who can not only give to them their complete and uninterrupted attention but who can also develop explicit skills requisite for their solution. Our modern large corporations need more than the intuitive and "below-the-belt" insight of a few gifted people. They need to introduce in their organizations a skill in human relations comparable to the skill which they introduce when they hire an engineer. And as a very large part of this skill, there is required on the part of the group charged with this responsibility a "sense of the whole," a concept of the interrelatedness of the phenomena with which they are trying to deal.

This is our concept of adequate personnel management. For

us, adequate personnel management is as much dependent upon a skill of diagnosing human situations as upon a plan or policy. Our plea is for the explicit recognition and systematic application of a specialty which is addressing itself to the adequate diagnosis and understanding of the actual human situations in a business organization.

HOW CAN THE SKILL OF DIAGNOSING HUMAN SITUATIONS BE DEVELOPED?

There are three elements in the development of such a skill which have been well stated by Dr. L. J. Henderson,[2] He says:

> In the complex business of living as in medicine *both* theory and practice are necessary conditions of understanding, and the method of Hippocrates is the only method that has ever succeeded widely and generally. The first element of that method is hard, persistent, intelligent, responsible, unremitting labor in the sick room, not in the library: the complete adaptation of the doctor to his task, an adaptation that is far from being merely intellectual. The second element of that method is accurate observation of things and events, selection, guided by judgment born of familiarity and experience, of the salient and the recurrent phenomena, and their classification and methodical exploitation. The third element of that method is the judicious construction of a theory — not a philosophical theory, nor a grand effort of the imagination, nor a quasi-religious dogma, but a modest pedestrian affair or perhaps I had better say, a useful walking-stick to help on the way — and the use thereof. All this may be summed up in a word: The physician must have, first, intimate, habitual, intuitive familiarity with things; secondly, systematic knowledge of things; and thirdly, an effective way of thinking about things.

Let me paraphrase what Dr. Henderson says for our particular problem. In large-scale industry today adequate personnel management requires a group of people who can give their complete and uninterrupted attention to the development of a skill of handling particular human problems which arise in

[2] *Three Lectures on Concrete Sociology*, p. 6.

their particular organizations. The development of such a skill would require, first, hard, persistent, intelligent, responsible, unremitting labor in the shops among employees at the work level, not in an office on the top floor. Only in this way can be obtained an intimate, habitual, intuitive familiarity with the way workers do behave — not how they "ought to" behave or are represented as behaving by those on the top floor. The second element in the development of the skill would require a careful search for simple uniformities which may appear among the facts that are collected and roughly classified. The third step in the development of the skill would be to construct a simple way of thinking about individuals and their relations to one another in a business organization. This way of thinking would be a modest affair which would help in obtaining more facts and in making practice more effective.

This approach is no short cut to success. It is a slow, laborious route; but it is the same route which has been followed for the past three hundred years in dealing with our physical world and which has resulted in such tremendous advances in the form of electric lights, telephones, radios, automobiles. This does not mean, however, that we in the personnel field have to wait three hundred years in order to get results. A very modest and simple beginning in the direction outlined by Dr. Henderson might bring almost at once fairly satisfying results in the three areas of human problems previously outlined. In fact it seems to me that a sufficient body of knowledge already exists in terms of which a simple theory can be constructed, the application of which would make personnel practice more effective in handling these three problems and ultimately in securing coöperation.

A USEFUL WAY OF THINKING ABOUT INDIVIDUALS IN A BUSINESS ORGANIZATION

What is the Individual Bringing to the Work Situation?

Probably the first step in the development of such a theory would be to have a simple way of thinking about the individuals in a business organization. In one sense, each person is unique. Each is bringing to the job situation certain attitudes, beliefs, and ways of life, as well as certain skills, technical, social, and logical. In terms of his previous experience, each person has certain hopes and expectations of his job situation.

What are some of these demands which he is making of his job? Obviously, the answer is not simple. It varies from person to person depending upon the individual's previous background and experience. Some people more than others are eager for recognition in the form of advancement. Some more than others are eager for recognition in the size of the pay check. But most of us want social recognition in one form or another. Most of us want the satisfaction that comes from being accepted and recognized as a person of worth by our friends and associates and the feeling of security that comes from being a member of a group. We want to have a skill that is socially recognized as useful. We want tangible evidence of our importance to our fellow men. However, the particular hopes and fears, the particular social values, which each person brings to the situation vary with each individual, depending upon his background and previous experience. This is one aspect of the human organization of which any skilled administrator is aware — the particularity and uniqueness of each individual in his organization — a factor which on occasions it may be very important for him to take into account.

But to overstress the differences among the individuals who make up a business organization would be to miss some of the common ties which bind men in collaborative activity, and which, if not present, make collaboration impossible. Although, in a sense, each individual in the organization is unique and different, it is also true that each person in this country has gone through a certain cultural sieve which gives him something in common with his fellow men. Parents, particularly those who were born in this country, have transmitted the common cultural heritage of this country to their children. Through participation in common educational, religious, and political associations they have been brought up to share certain common values, to have common hopes, faiths, and standards of living. These experiences help to fit them for social living and prepare them for coöperation. Without some such common feelings and sentiments, effective coöperation is impossible. Any administrator is assuming, sometimes more than he realizes, that the people who come to his organization have already been socially conditioned in a fashion which has prepared them for coöperation. This cannot always be assumed. Sometimes more assistance than that provided by the parents or the formal educational system needs to be given after the person has gone to work.

What is the Work Situation Demanding of the Individual?

In developing our conception of the individual in a business organization, it is well to remember that each person not only has a past, but is also working in a present situation. He is working under particular conditions, associating with particular people. These associations are not of a hit-or-miss character. They are composed of people who have certain defined and accepted relations to one another. In his present situation, there are also certain standards to which the individual has to conform — standards of performance regarding the quantity and quality of work he does and standards of personal conduct. Pressure is put upon him to behave in a certain way, to have certain loyalties, to hold certain beliefs. Some of these pressures are in the form of law and prescribed rules of behavior; some of them are in the form of customary ways of doing things.

It is also well to remember that the individual's present situation is wider than his immediate work situation. He is also associating with people outside of work. He may have a family and belong to numerous associations in the community to which he is contributing his services, in most cases not for monetary gain. In this situation outside of work he is also submitted to pressures of one kind or another — to be a dutiful father and husband, to be a loyal citizen.

What is the Resulting Equilibrium?

It can be seen that a person's satisfactions or dissatisfactions are relative to (1) the demands he is bringing to the situation, and (2) the demands the situation is making of him. In order to maintain his equilibrium he has to resolve these two sets of pressures. If there is too big a gap between the social satisfaction which he is asking from his job and the social satisfaction he is getting from his job, he has a grievance. If he is bringing to his situation a demand for recognition which his present job cannot satisfy, he becomes discontented. If he is unable to fulfill the technical requirements of the job, he may become dissatisfied; then the supervisor also has a grievance. If he cannot meet the social requirements of the job and cannot adjust himself to the group, he becomes dissatisfied and often, as a result, cannot fulfill the technical requirements.

This constant adjustment between what is being asked of the individual and what he is asking of the situation is a simple framework in which our thought can be set when handling people in a business organization. Each person himself is continuously trying to resolve these two tendencies but sometimes he needs to be helped: either (1) in the direction of modifying his demands so that they can be better realized in the present situation, or (2) by changing the present situation so as to allow for the fulfillment of the normal demands he is making of his work, or (3) both.

It should be noted that this way of thinking about individuals in a business organization does not tell us in particular what any person is like or what his situation is. It only gives us a useful set of ideas — a framework in which our thought can be set — when we are confronted with a particular person and want to find out what his situation is. It suggests the kind of material that is needed, where to look, and how to go about making a diagnosis.

A USEFUL WAY OF THINKING ABOUT THE INTERACTIONS OF INDIVIDUALS IN A BUSINESS ORGANIZATION

What are the Formal Patterns of Behavior in a Group?

The second step in the development of a theory for more effective personnel practice involves the construction of a simple way of conceiving of the interactions of individuals in a business organization. We started this process in the last section when we considered some of the elements of the work situation to which the individual brings his hopes and fears and to which he has to conform. Let us continue with this analysis. The human organization of a business concern is made up of more than a plurality of isolated, atomic individuals. These different individuals also have different relations to one another. Some of these relations are prescribed; some of them become well accepted and firmly established in the routines of the group; some remain more transitory in character. But, as a result of these interactions, a social structure arises — a complex network of relations, some of which endure regardless of the individuals who come and go.

If we look at the total personnel of a business organization, then, we find that it can be divided and subdivided into groups, each group being identified with a function related to the economic purpose of the total enterprise. Each person is contributing his services to the technical purpose of the smaller group of which he is a part. This part of the human organization is generally shown on an organization chart. It is the formal aspect of the human organization. The formal organization defines what the relations of people to one another should be in order that the economic purpose be efficiently achieved. It says who reports to whom; it prescribes the formal channels of communication and authority. This is one aspect of the working environment to which the individual has to relate himself — the formal patterns of behavior prescribed by the formal organization.

What are the Informal Patterns of Behavior in a Group?

But there is more to the human organization than what has been formalized or explicitly recognized. Individuals in their associations with one another build up personal relations. They form into social groups. They elaborate and adopt certain norms of conduct, routines of behavior, and common ways of thinking. They come together in informal social groups within the formal framework of the company.

In any social group, whether it be large or small and regardless of the technical purpose it serves, there are certain common elements. There are certain beliefs which have the effect of making each individual feel an integral part of the social group and which make the group appear as a single unit. There is a certain set of attitudes or norms, codes and routines of behavior by means of which the members are automatically able to work together.

If we look at the human organization of any business enterprise, we find, first, groups of people formally organized, each group having its technical and economic purpose. However, we also find that these groups, as well as many others not formally recognized, have their own informal codes of behavior and their own sentiments in terms of which the behavior of their members is regulated and controlled.

These informal organizations have a very healthy and normal function in any business organization. They give people who are members of such organizations a feeling of security, a feeling of belonging, and a feeling of being part of something. Much of the effective working together of people is dependent upon informal routines and codes of behavior, because without them any organization can be maintained only by force. Only with them is there an effective basis for collaboration. They function for the individual in two ways: the individual who subordinates himself to group codes of behavior obtains, on the one hand, certain feelings of security and, on the other, certain feelings of social satisfaction. It is well to remember, then, that informal organization is not "bad." On the contrary, it makes for healthy social life.

What are the Major Schemes in Terms of Which Individuals are being Evaluated?

Associated with both the formal and informal organizations are two sets of beliefs and ideas in terms of which people are being evaluated: (1) the standards prescribed by the formal organization; (2) the codes of behavior prescribed by the informal organization. Some of these evaluational schemes are much more explicit than others. Those of the formal organization are in general more logically explicit and articulate than those of the informal organization, but they are not for that reason more powerful in their effects than those of the informal organization. The sentiments underlying the evaluations made by the informal organization are often very powerful determinants of human behavior. The result may be that a worker feels worse to be judged a "rate buster" by his fellow workers than to be judged a "poor worker" by his supervisor. And he may behave accordingly.

What is the Resulting Equilibrium?

Here are three variables in terms of which problems relating to balance in the internal organization of a business concern can be simply diagnosed: (1) the formal patterns of behavior, (2) the informal patterns of behavior, and (3) evaluational schemes of both the formal and informal organizations in terms of which individuals are being judged. It should be noted that these variables do not tell us what the social situation is in particular, but they do tell us the major factors in terms of which a particular situation can be diagnosed. For example, they allow us to see what is happening to people in their relations to one another when technical changes are introduced, when a person is transferred from one department to another, or when a person is promoted or demoted from one job to another. In the case of the individual, they allow us to specify the particular social situation at work—the social structure, both formal and informal—to which the individual has to conform.

But more important still, they allow us to see the interrelated character of the human problems in any business organization. We begin to see among these three variables a mutually dependent relation such that a change in any one is likely to be followed by changes in the others. We begin to see that we cannot change the formal patterns of behavior without affecting the informal patterns of behavior and, in turn, without affecting the criteria in terms of which people are being evaluated.

HOW CAN A CONDITION OF BALANCE BE MAINTAINED?

Let us now see how this simple theory can help to make personnel practice more effective in handling the three major human problems originally defined. A business organization can be conceived of as having a social structure through which individuals are moving in time and place. This social structure is characterized by patterns of behavior with their associated sentiments, values, and beliefs. In most business organizations this social structure becomes in time relatively stable. In fact, in order to function effectively, it requires a certain stability. But once this stability is achieved it resists change. Certain parts of the structure, of course, can be changed more rapidly than others; but if, in general, changes are not too rapid, the equilibrium remains fairly stable.

To the social structure of a business organization individuals are bringing certain hopes and expectations, demands which arise from their past experiences and present social situations outside of work. Within the social structure the individual hopes to fulfill his demands; and through it he can obtain human satisfactions which make him willing to coöperate through contributing his services to the economic objective. Through the social structure he can obtain recognition, security, new experiences, and the satisfactions that come from coöperation itself. It becomes, therefore, very important to see that a condition of balance obtains; to see that within the social structure serious dislocations do not occur because important considerations are unwittingly ignored.

Now local conditions of unbalance may arise from a number of different sources. The too-rapid introduction into a group of a technical change which interferes too violently with the workers' customary ways of doing things may produce a local condition of unbalance. Promotions which do not take into account the sentiments of the informal group from which the promotion was made may produce such an unbalance. The same applies to many of the personnel functions — hiring, up-grading, downgrading, transferring, etc. All these functions, if performed with neglect or ignorance of the existing patterns of behavior and their associated sentiments and beliefs, may produce local conditions of unbalance. The faulty orientations of supervisors to their jobs may produce a local condition of unbalance. Faulty or inadequate schemes of evaluation also may have the same consequence for particular individuals and groups. If these sources of interference can be detected, adequately diagnosed, and treated in time, local conditions of unbalance can be corrected. But if they are allowed to remain, they tend to grow into a more widespread condition of unbalance affecting the total personnel of the organization. This general disequilibrium will manifest itself in an unbalanced relation of groups such that one group in the organization separates itself out in opposition to the remainder.

The Conditions under Which an Unbalance is More Likely to Occur

By analyzing the conditions under which an unbalance is more likely to occur we begin to see the mutually dependent set of relations into which the problem resolves. We note first that any industrial or business concern is made up of groups, each group with its own code of behavior and sentiments. We see that it is important that no one group has a code of behavior too much at variance with the economic objectives of the company as a whole. However, we also note that processes making for differentiation are present in the social organization of any business concern — age, service, occupation, rank. We realize that those processes tending to make for differentiation must be offset by equally strong integrating processes. Although in the modern industrial setting there seems to be a marked tendency for the employee group to separate itself out in opposition to the remainder of the organization, this is more likely when

(1) there are many processes which are tending to differentiate this group from all others and there is little movement from this group into other groups,

(2) there is a tendency to eliminate those social processes at the work level which differentiate the workers themselves from one another,

(3) the opportunities for differentiation in terms of management standards exclude or run counter to the opportunities for differentiation in terms of the conventions of ordinary social living,

(4) management is out of touch with the sentiments of the worker and frequently has to act in ignorance of these sentiments; consequently, management practices often collide with the sentiments of the employees, with the result that the employees form an informal protective organization against such practices.

Now it can be seen that there are many tendencies in modern industry in this very direction. Employee groups are frequently sharply differentiated from office groups, technical groups, and the supervisory organization, in terms of working conditions, methods of work, and standards of performance. On no group has there been so much work done in the direction of measuring the quantity and quality of performance and paying in accordance with it. Although such processes have allowed for differentiations among the working force, these differentiations have all been in terms of measurable abstractions — output, cost, quotas, standards of performance of one kind or another — that evaluate the contribution of employees to the economic purpose of the organization. The modern industrial setting tends therefore to maximize those evaluations which differentiate people in terms of efficiency and to minimize those evaluations which differentiate people in terms of the conventions of ordinary social life.

Now the implications of this tendency are rather interesting. First, what may it imply for advancement through the organization? May it mean that the person who is successful in advancing through the organization is likely to be better oriented to the abstractions relating to efficiency than to the conventions of ordinary social living? And what effect may this have upon his capacity to deal with people and to secure their collaboration?

But perhaps more interesting still, what may it imply for those people who have never advanced very far but have stayed at the bottom or at the lower levels of the organization? Are they likely to resent being constantly evaluated in terms which perhaps symbolize "failure"? Might they welcome the opportunity for differentiations which express the human values residing in their personal interrelations? If deprived of the opportunity for such differentiations, might they tend to seek associations which would provide them? Might they get this kind of human satisfaction through their union activities—the satisfaction of belonging to a group where they will be evaluated more in the terms of social conventions than in the terms of logics of efficiency? May this opportunity for social participation be as important to some of its members as the formal purpose for which a union is organized?

But these speculations, although interesting, are fruitless when indulged in apart from particular business organizations. In most business organizations, both evaluational systems are at work: those which are evaluating people in terms of standards of performance and those which are evaluating them in terms of social codes of behavior. But in some organizations, they work at cross purposes, particularly if it is assumed that mechanisms which are useful for the attainment of the object of the coöperation will, at the same time, take into account, deal satisfactorily with, and apply to the concrete coöperative situation. Many of these evaluational schemes overemphasize the evaluation of separate individuals and underemphasize the evaluation of situations. They assume that the individual can be evaluated apart from his relations to other people. They tend to treat the employees as a horde of unrelated individuals, each having certain qualities and characteristics.

This situation was well illustrated in a sales department of a department store studied by our group. Twice a year each employee was given a "job review," in which his work for the past six months was critically examined by a board of three people, and suggestions were made as to how his performance might be improved. Each individual was evaluated in and by himself. In terms of certain criteria, he learned his strengths and shortcomings and where he stood in the eyes of his supervisors. Now this department had a high morale; this was the reputation it enjoyed in the store. A casual observation revealed numerous evidences of social solidarity. In many respects, it resembled a small town. Many different kinds of merchandise were sold. Each person had a definite social function and place. Each person was an expert in some small area. Group recognition was granted to each special skill. Everyone recognized that Bill knew birds, Tom knew how to mix paints, etc. The department had its saga and its traditions. It had its "railroad tracks" and the small-town distinctions attaching to them. It had its small-town characters, among them the prankster, the bad boy, the blow-hard, and the busybody; but each was accepted for what he was and for the part he played in the total social life of the group. In this department, to compare two salespeople in terms of management's logics was a pointless business. To the people intimately concerned, it did not make sense — no more sense than it would make to compare on some abstract scale the different roles of the personalities of a small town. In such a situation it looked to the outside observer as if these "job reviews" were satisfying management's desire to appear logical and rational in its dispensations of justice rather than satisfying the desires of the employees. In spite of, rather than with the assistance of, top management this group preserved its social integrity and morale.

HOW TO KEEP CLEAR THE CHANNELS OF COMMUNICATION

It can be seen that conditions of unbalance arise in part because of a failure to keep clear the channels of communication. As a result, management is out of touch with the concrete situations at the work level. The point of view we are suggesting would help in specifying, diagnosing, and treating many blockages in the channels of communication. Some of them arise because of faulty orientations and inadequate human evaluations on the part of supervisors. In work situations where there exists a considerable discrepancy between the way the situation is and the way it should be, not because of any fault of the supervisor but because of conditions outside of his control, a supervisor is frequently put into a position of giving lip service to a point of view which it would be suicidal for him to practice. In such a situation of insecurity it is not unlikely that he will edit everything that he passes up the line. Some supervisors can communicate more easily to their superiors or get their communications more readily accepted when their communications are in terms of the usual criteria of efficiency rather than in terms of the informal social processes within their groups. The buyer in the sales department above mentioned was in this difficulty. The more we observed his behavior the more we were impressed with the unusually good job he was doing in securing the collaboration of his working force. He knew them all — their situations both inside and outside of work — and he handled them accordingly. But to explain what he did in terms of certain abstractions from the total situation was exceedingly difficult. It would have sounded more like "monkey business" than "business as usual." As a result, no one realized what a good job he was doing; and top management continued to make decisions in its ivory tower.

The problems of communication that arise in relations of supervisors to employees, as well as in relations that obtain between various levels of the supervisory structure, are difficult to diagnose and difficult to correct in a simple and direct manner. What they require more than anything else, however, is intelligent understanding. But who in our business organizations has the time and the skill to do this?

HOW TO IMPROVE INDIVIDUAL WORK EFFECTIVENESS

As we have both said and implied frequently, it is our contention that what is needed more than anything else in business organizations is a skill in the diagnosis and treatment of human situations practiced by a group who can give their full and uninterrupted attention to the task. It is sheer folly to think that things can be fixed up human-wise once and for all. When an engineer is hired by an automobile manufacturer, let us say, he is not expected to design the best car for all time. He is only expected to build the best car he knows how to build, here and now, under certain limiting conditions. For him, because he has a skill, there is never the "best" car. There is always a better car to be built tomorrow. There is only the "best" car built in this particular year.

Curiously enough, this is not what is expected from a human relations expert. He is expected to produce a foolproof system, plan, or panacea, something which will solve human problems for all time, and then to disappear as quickly as possible from the scene of his iniquity. No automobile manufacturer would be insulted or hurt if it were suggested that this year's model of his product could be improved; yet he resents any implication that all is not what it might be in the area of human relations. He would lead us to believe that either everything is perfect or there is a strike. Just because the employees of a plant are not striking, everything in the human relations area is entirely satisfactory.

The point of view we are recommending runs quite counter to this. It suggests that in any business organization there are tensions and strains. Interferences of one kind or another may arise which will make for conditions of human unbalance. These interferences and resulting unbalances have to be detected, diagnosed, and dealt with at the time and place in which they occur. Systems of communication cannot be made perfect for all time. Supervisors cannot be harangued or "educated" for all time into being as good at the receiving end as at the transmitting end of the communication system. Employees cannot be harangued or "educated" for all time into understanding the logical and economic purposes of the top management group. Local interferences will and do arise. The channels of communication can and do become blocked.

Ultimately, the dissatisfied individual or disturbing employee or supervisor has to be dealt with. Discharging him or transferring him to some spot where he can do less harm — the personnel organization, for example — is sometimes not the solution. What he may need is just a little help in the direction of understanding his situation. Maybe it is a problem of orientation: Maybe he has just been moved from one department to another and he needs time and understanding to reorient himself to his new situation — not only to the technical requirements of the job, but also to the norms of conduct of the new work group to which he has been assigned. Maybe he has, without quite realizing it, just grown older and has moved from one age or service group to another and must reorient himself to the changes in his relations with older and younger groups.

Perhaps it is a problem of evaluation: Maybe the individual is incorrectly evaluating himself or the situation of which he is a part. Maybe he is making a faulty evaluation of his workers or supervisors. This is leading him to inappropriate decisions and actions. These incorrect or inadequate evaluations are of the utmost importance in the successful functioning of the concern, since they relate not only to the work satisfactions of the individual but also to the selection of people for promotion and, indeed, to all the major decisions made by employees, supervisors, and management.

Our solution for inadequate orientations and evaluations on the part of both workers and supervisors is clear. They can be handled only on the spot; not by pieces of paper emanating from the top floor. For their adequate treatment, a skill of diagnosis is involved: a skill of understanding a concrete human total situation, of analyzing a complex human phenomenon into those elements which have produced it, analogous to the skill of the medical diagnostician who can go from the symptoms to the realities behind them. It is not a skill of juggling with words and abstractions. It addresses itself to somebody in the concrete, not to somebody or anybody but nobody in particular. It is a skill which is trying to discover what is present in some particular human situation in some particular place at some particular time. It is not interested in what is on a person's mind in general; it is interested in what is on some one person's mind — a person who has had a particular personal history, who was brought up in a particular family which had particular relations to the community, who, as a result of this particular social conditioning, comes to his job with particular hopes and fears and sentiments. Moreover, this person's job is in some particular place in the factory, which brings him into association with particular persons and groups of people; that is, he is in a particular social setting which is making particular demands of him and, as a result of the particular demands which the job is making of him and the particular demands which he is making of the job, there is a particular kind of equilibrium or disequilibrium.

CONCLUSION

There is one very important consequence which follows from the introduction of such a skill as I suggest. It adds to the two major evaluational systems in a business organization another very important, useful, and necessary type of evaluation. These three evaluations are:

(1) The evaluation of the behavior of an individual in terms of certain abstract logics and standards relating to performance and efficiency. This kind of *"individual" evaluation* is very common in business organizations.

(2) The evaluation of the behavior of an individual in terms of certain socially accepted codes and norms of conduct. This kind of *"social" evaluation* is very common and is going on all the time in the community as well as in business organizations. It goes on among equals as well as between superiors and subordinates.

(3) The evaluation which is trying to understand why a person behaves the way he does in terms of his *total situation.* This kind of *"situational" evaluation,* welcomed by most people, is rare in the community or in business. It is probably trite to point out that people usually want to be "understood" instead of always being "judged" by their superiors.

In conclusion, then, in our opinion, the personnel management of a particular business organization is adequate when

(1) it introduces in its own organization a skill of diagnosing human situations — not some pious platitudes or "wheezes" on how to treat employees *in general;*

(2) by means of this skill, it commits itself to the continuous process of studying the human situations — both individual and group — within its own organization;

(3) it tries to secure the collaboration of its employees by running its human affairs in terms of what it learns and discovers about its own organization;

(4) it learns that what is important to particular employees exists in its own back yard — not in university libraries or in the minds of university professors.

PART II

CHAPTER VIII

CONCERNING PEOPLE WHO DEAL WITH COÖPERATIVE PHENOMENA

IN EACH preceding chapter three points were being made in one form or another, sometimes directly and sometimes by implication:

(1) Administrators, their staffs, and line assistants deal with coöperative phenomena,[1] some more than others and some more successfully than others. Yet they do not often have an explicit frame in which their thought is set and in terms of which they can conveniently operate upon this class of phenomena.

(2) For this class of phenomena, convenient and useful working hypotheses and methods can be formulated; useful generalizations can be made. In short these phenomena constitute a legitimate field of inquiry in their own right.

(3) Social science has an important contribution to make to business administration in this area; not only does some useful knowledge now exist, but a great advance in the theory and practice of handling coöperative phenomena can be made by further inquiry, study, and research.

These points will provide the structure for this and the following chapters. Here we shall present businessmen to social scientists. We shall try to show social scientists that in business organizations coöperative phenomena do exist; that

[1] The phrase "coöperative phenomena" will be used to refer to concrete events involving the interactions of two or more persons in a system of coördinated activities. Cf. Chester I. Barnard's definition of formal organization in *The Functions of the Executive* (Cambridge: Harvard University Press, 1938), p. 73. It should be remembered that the word "coöperative" says nothing about the content of the interaction.

certain people, called "administrators" or "executives," do handle such phenomena daily; and that some of them do an extraordinarily good job. Therefore, before talking about "morale" on a national or international scale, might it not be wise to look at people who are daily dealing with the phenomena to which this word refers and see what they do, or do not do, in securing the coöperation of the individuals and groups they "administer"? In Chapter IX, we shall present social scientists to businessmen. If businessmen deal with and social scientists theorize about coöperative phenomena, do the theories of the latter bear any relation to the practice of the former? If so, what theories do and what theories do not? In the final chapter, we shall attempt to see what emerges as a useful working hypothesis for conceiving of the practice of administration on the one hand and of "morale" on the other.

THE RELATION OF THEORY TO PRACTICE

It is a curious fact that there are certain areas of endeavor where those who teach do not practice and those who practice do not teach.[2] In general, the skillful practitioners of business do not teach "economics" or "business" in our universities. Likewise, in general, those who teach economics in our universities do not practice business. Teachers of "government" do not often practice the skills of the politician or statesman; politicians or statesmen seldom teach government. This is not true in the fields of medicine or engineering. Here, more often than not, the men who teach are also practicing the skills they are teaching.

It is also interesting and profitable to note that in areas where those who practice do not teach and those who teach do

[2] Aristotle made these observations some two thousand years ago. See *Nicomachean Ethics*, Everyman's Edition, Book X, pp. 260–261. They have been amplified and developed by Dr. L. J. Henderson in his *Three Lectures on Concrete Sociology* (privately distributed) as an introduction to statements very similar to those which follow.

not practice, knowledge has not advanced very far; whereas in areas where those who teach are practicing the skills they teach, knowledge has advanced very far. For example, what Aristotle said some two thousand years ago about politics makes as much sense today as it did then. However, what the Greeks said about medicine two thousand years ago would sound like gibberish to the modern medical student. No medical student today in order to practice medicine skillfully needs to know the medical opinions of the Greeks. Likewise, chemistry, physics, and engineering have progressed far since the days of the Greeks. It would seem fair to conclude, then, that knowledge has advanced more rapidly in those areas where those who teach are also practicing the skills they teach. This is just another way of saying that knowledge has advanced more rapidly where theory and practice have gone hand in hand.

In these remarks it should be noted that, although the importance of practice has been emphasized, the need of theory has not been depreciated. Rather, it will be our contention that, although theory without practice is futile speculation, practice without theory is incommunicable. The two should be cultivated together if we are to learn by experience and be able to communicate what we learn.

MEN WHO PRACTICE SKILLFULLY BUT DO NOT CARE TO THEORIZE ABOUT IT

By applying these distinctions to the area of human management in business, we are enabled to make a number of obvious statements. In business today there are people who are exceedingly skillful in handling human relations. They are key men in the direction of group effort. Their importance to the organizations they serve lies primarily in their ability to secure the coöperation of individuals in attaining the technological purposes of the group. Such men may bear a number of different titles (supervisors, administrators, executives, group leaders, foremen, vice presidents, presidents), or they may bear no titles at all. Moreover, the bearing of any of these titles or labels offers no guarantee in itself with regard to the efficient performance of this function. Nevertheless, regardless of label, the worthwhileness of those who effectively perform the function of securing coöperative effort is intuitively recognized and granted by those intimately associated with the situation. Of the need and importance of such people there is little question. No logical coördination of functions can supplant the need for the more social skills of securing coöperative effort which certain men practice effectively in the concrete work situation.

Skillful practitioners, however, often cannot state their skills explicitly. Unlike the more logical or technical skills, these are embedded in the individual and his concrete experience. They are personal, empirical, and intuitive. Many of these men shun talking about or generalizing about their skills. They like to deal with concrete situations; their thinking is likely to be syncretistic and ineffable. Put them in charge of a group of men doing a definite job, and they come to life. Ask them to relate how they handled a particular problem, and they show uncanny insight. Put them on a platform and ask them to discuss the principles of managing men, and they grow red in the face and indulge in endless wheezes about human nature in general.

For these men when operating in their own milieu we have the profoundest admiration and respect. To judge them in a context alien to their ability is to misjudge entirely the extraordinary skills they possess. Many of our generalizations merely make explicit what these men intuitively know and practice — this has been said frequently in the preceding chapters. But it is well to recognize the limitations of these men. They cannot explicitly communicate their skills to others. Their skills leave the organization with them when they die or retire. They are the so-called "practical" men who depreciate "theory," although they do not realize how much theorizing of a crude sort they often do.

MEN WITH SPECIALIZED SKILLS RELATING TO MANAGEMENT PRACTICE

There are other men in modern rationalized business, generally in staff positions, who are much more articulate with regard to the skills they practice. They include not only people who are interested in improving the product and method of manufacture — physicists, chemists, metallurgists, pharmacologists, and engineers of one kind or another — but also people who are interested in various "control" devices to secure the effective functioning of the enterprise — economists, lawyers, cost accountants, market analysts, statisticians, time and motion study men, personnel men, industrial engineers, production control men, wage incentive system experts.

Unlike the intuitive leaders of men, these men, in general, are much better able to state what they are doing. Some of them recognize quite clearly the limited class of phenomena to which their areas of specialization relate. With regard to the utility of these different specialist groups in the total effective functioning of a business organization there is no question. Each has contributed valuable skills and techniques to the development of modern business. Collectively they have created new types of economic organizations for which there is no historical parallel. Considered in terms of the fulfillment of their economic purpose of producing and distributing goods effectively, or in terms of the kinds, the quality, and the quantity of goods produced, or in terms of the mechanical inventions and economic knowledge they have directly or indirectly promoted, these organizations far surpass anything which could have been expected in the early part of the nineteenth century.

Nothing comparable to this advance in knowledge and achievement has gone on in the area of human collaboration.

In comparison, very little is yet known about how to secure the coöperation of people in attaining the economic purposes of modern business enterprises. There is little evidence which would lead us to believe that in them there has been achieved any more human satisfaction, happiness, or "morale" than in more primitive types of economic organization. Within some of them much strife and human privation still exist.

In order to shed some light on this vivid but unfortunate comparison, in each chapter in Part I an attempt was made, in some form, to distinguish between the two-fold functions that exist in any coöperative activity: (1) the function of securing the common collective purpose for which the organization exists, and (2) the function of securing the whole-hearted services of individuals in attaining this coöperative purpose.[8] In a business organization these two functions are: (1) that of producing and distributing effectively a product, and (2) that of securing the coöperation of individuals in attaining that purpose. The fulfillment of the second function implies that in giving their services to the common purpose people obtain satisfactions which make them willing to coöperate. These two functions are, of course, interrelated in the long run: both functions must be fulfilled if the organization is to endure.

In terms of this distinction, we can understand better the contributions of the different specialist groups to business. Most of them have made invaluable contributions in the direction of stating the necessary conditions for effective technical production and distribution of goods. Their contributions in the direction of stating the conditions for meaningful human association at work, however, are much more questionable. The reasons why this is so require more analysis. To begin with, let us divide these specialist groups into two subclasses: (1) those in whose fields of specialization coöperative phe-

[8] These very important distinctions are made by Barnard, *The Functions of the Executive*, pp. 55–61.

nomena are not involved and therefore can be conveniently ignored, and (2) those in whose fields of specialization coöperative phenomena are involved and therefore cannot be conveniently ignored.

SPECIALISTS WHOSE FIELDS DO NOT INVOLVE COÖPERATIVE PHENOMENA

Among members of the first group, composed of physicists, chemists, mechanical, civil, chemical engineers, and so on, certain characteristics are evident. Most of them are concerned with a particular, limited class of phenomena. The events with which their specialization is concerned do not involve the interactions of persons. They have a useful way of thinking about and a simple method of dealing with their own class of phenomena. Within this area their judgments are likely to be sound. Outside it their judgments are more questionable. Some of them recognize quite clearly this limitation. They do not want to be concerned with the human factor; they want to design the best tool, the best machine to accomplish certain technical purposes. Whether or not the introduction of this tool or machine will involve the layoff of certain employees, quite rightly, is not their concern as engineers. Their contribution, in terms of the skill they practice, is to improve from a technical standpoint the performance or utility of a machine, a tool, or a product.

These men are invaluable to the administrator in any industrial organization. Within their area of specialization, they have come to enjoy a certain autonomy. No administrator would attempt to dictate to them their theories or skills or judgments within their area of competency. In this consists the prestige they rightfully enjoy in most business organizations. To them we owe the new and powerful technology of modern industry. To criticize them for failing to take into account the social consequences of their own discipline is absurd. When, therefore, we describe some of the human consequences at the work level of technical changes brought about by engineers, this is not intended as a criticism of this group. Bringing into coöperative relation their particular skills with other skills is not their function; it is a quite different function performed by other groups in the organization.

The virtue of the engineers [4] is that, for the most part, they know what they are doing and what they are talking about in their own fields. They have a strong appreciation of "fact" and "logic," but, more important still, they are likely to know within their own area what they do not know. As a result, with their blunt and direct remarks, they provide a welcome relief to some business conferences. Their sense of fact and logic, however, sometimes has a way of making for difficulties in their human associations. For them everything is likely to be fact or error. When they participate in or deal with phenomena to which these two categories do not so clearly apply, they are likely to go off the deep end.

Were it not that in a business organization engineers have to coöperate with other groups and that sometimes engineers move into administrative positions, this difficulty in understanding the nature of coöperative phenomena would make no difference. However, when an engineer becomes an administrator he becomes, whether he likes it or not, concerned with a class of phenomena to which his former specialty has no relevance. Some engineers recognize this and accommodate themselves accordingly; others do not — they continue to handle coöperative phenomena as if they were handling a machine, more often than not with disastrous results. But the point we are trying to make here can be better stated with

[4] This label is being used here merely as a convenient way of referring to people who effectively practice a skill relating to events that do not involve the interactions of persons. It is well to remember that there may be some people in business who have this label but who are not practicing the skill here defined.

regard to the second group of specialists — those in whose area of specialization the interactions of persons cannot be conveniently disregarded.

SPECIALISTS WHOSE FIELDS DO INVOLVE COÖPERATIVE PHENOMENA

If things in this world were simple, it would seem that, just as the administrator has persons with clear-cut specialties to aid him in handling noncoöperative phenomena, so he would have persons with other clear-cut specialties to aid him in dealing with the coöperative phenomena with which he is also concerned. But here things become complex and confused, for there are a number of specialties in business whose relation to a particular class of phenomena is not so clear. Although at times, by abstraction, a certain aspect may be conveniently separated out for independent and special study, the matrix from which this abstraction is made generally involves the interactions of people. At times, particularly when these abstractions are applied to the concrete situation, the interactions of people may be the most important variables. As a result, the working hypotheses of these specialists, particularly on their applied side, must be far less clear, distinct, and well formulated than in the more highly developed and exact engineering sciences. There is no simple way of thinking about or putting together the complicated events involved, and there is equally no simple method of dealing with them.

Many of the techniques and specialties whose purpose is to improve the efficiency of workers fall into this category. They relate in part to the securing of the economic purpose of the total organization and in part to the securing of the coöperation of individuals in attaining that purpose. Motion economy offers a good example. In a certain sense, there is a way in which a worker can assemble a certain number of piece parts with the fewest number of motions. By abstraction, this aspect of the worker's environment can be separated out for individual study. For many purposes, it is a convenient and useful abstraction to make, and there is no question that in terms of it increases in efficiency can and have been made.

However, there is another aspect of the application of this abstraction which cannot be quite ignored: To what extent does the application of motion economy secure the coöperation of individuals? Is it "better" to have a worker who is efficient from the point of view of motion economy but dissatisfied as a person; or is it "better" to have a worker who is happy but not so efficient from the point of view of motion economy? These are clearly rhetorical questions. They have served their purpose if they show distinctly that in the application of motion economy to concrete work situations two different classes of phenomena are involved. The application of the most economical way of performing certain operations to concrete work situations involves individuals in their relations to one another. It involves attitudes, feelings, and sentiments. At times, these factors cannot be conveniently disregarded, as any motion economy expert in practice recognizes. From a technical standpoint, many things in business can be done more efficiently; but if in the process of introducing changes toward this end a strike is produced, what do we mean by "efficiency"?

Measuring the Performance of Employees

It is unfortunate that in business today we have one word, "efficiency," to apply to two quite different aspects of coöperative behavior. One is concerned with the attainment of the object of the coöperation, the other with the fulfillment of human satisfaction.[5] To use one word for these two aspects allows us to slip from one class to another class of phenomena without realizing that we are doing so. It allows us frequently

[5] Barnard made an important contribution by using two different words—"effective" and "efficient"—for these two aspects of coöperative behavior, *The Functions of the Executive*, pp. 55–61.

to have our cake and eat it too. Nowhere is this more apparent than in trying to measure the performance of different people in a business organization — workers, salesmen, foremen. It is taken for granted in modern business that in order to perform equitably such operations as promotion, upgrading, payment, the performance of people should be measured. Otherwise, how can we tell whether a salesman or a worker or a foreman is doing a "good" job and is being rewarded equitably in terms of the job he is doing?

For our purposes it is needless to discuss the many different ways in which standards are set up or can be set up for assessing the performance of individuals. The difficulties of the problem become apparent when we try to visualize in the case of salesmen the many factors which must be taken into account in order that Quota 1 for Salesman 1 in Territory 1 with Population 1 with Economic Classes 1, 2, 3 can be compared with Quota 2 for Salesman 2 in Territory 2 with Population 2 with Economic Classes 4, 5, 6, so that the performance of Salesman 1 can be compared with the performance of Salesman 2 or that of each, in terms of his own quota, can be equitably measured. It is apparent that similar problems exist in measuring the performance of Foreman 1 with Workers 1, 2, 3, 4, 5, etc. doing Jobs 1, 2, 3, 4, 5, etc., at the Level of Business Activity 1, or at the Level of Business Activity 2, and the performance of Foreman 2 with Workers *a, b, c, d, e,* etc. doing Jobs *a, b, c, d, e,* etc., at the Level of Business Activity 3, or at the Level of Business Activity 4.

Let us say that by trial and error and by experiment and observation, and by now correcting for this and by now correcting for that, standards can be set up in terms of which an individual's performance can be measured. Let us even assume that all the environmental differences of Territory 1 of Salesman 1, which affect his performance but over which he has no control, have been taken into account. The question now is:

How is this standard going to be used by Salesman 1's boss — let us call him Sales Manager 1? It is assumed, of course, that the purpose of this standard is not merely to give Sales Manager 1 an aesthetic appreciation or a feeling of security that all is well in his territory because he knows how each individual stands in respect to everyone else. It is assumed that this standard is going to be used. But how is such a standard useful to him? Of course, it is agreed that he has now something in terms of which to assess Salesman 1's performance. However, it can be used by Sales Manager 1 in a number of different ways: to give Salesman 1 a bawling-out, a compliment, a raise, a promotion, a new territory, or to fire him. It can also be used as the occasion for an interview in order to find out why Salesman 1 is or is not coming up to his quota. Moreover, depending upon its use by Sales Manager 1, it may have different meanings to Salesmen 1, 2, 3, 4, 5, etc. It may act as a spur, as a whip, as a means of going to the boss for a raise or for a change in territory. Or it may be a symbol around which a salesman can organize any resentments or antagonisms to his superior or to the organization. He may think it unfair in that it is not taking into account the uniqueness of his territory — "that damned corner druggist."

Let us assume that during Week 1 Salesman 1 falls short of his quota. Let us say that during that week Salesman 1's wife was in the hospital, having just been operated upon for cancer. How does Sales Manager 1 take this factor into account? Does he even know about it? How does he get this kind of information anyway? Assume that he knows about it, what does he do? Does he say, "Hard luck, old man, better luck next week"?

Let us further assume that each week Salesman 1 has a hard-luck story. One week he is not feeling well; the next week the weather is bad; the next week something else unusual happens. What does the sales manager do? Argue each week with regard to each different excuse he makes? Fire him? If he fires him, does Sales Manager 1 have to take into consideration what effect this might have on the rest of his sales force? Or maybe he tries to find out what the matter is? If he takes this latter approach, how does he do this? Does he look at Salesman 1, at Salesman 1's territory, or at both? How does he consider Salesman 1, as a salesman who is incidentally a person, or as a person who has the label "salesman"? If he considers him as a person, does he consider him as a person who has always been a "man"? Or does he consider him as a man who was once a little boy who perhaps had ambitions of becoming President of the United States, or who was once a young man who spent his early life in Community 1 and who is now Salesman 1 in Corporation 1, doing his job in Territory 1, as well as the husband of Wife 1 with Children 1, 2, and 3 in Community 2?

Standards of Work Performance in Relation to Coöperative Phenomena

In citing these illustrations, we have been trying to suggest the complex situations which any person in an administrative position encounters. Any sales manager will intuitively know what we have been discussing in the above section. We have been trying to separate (1) a standard of performance which as an abstraction from a complex situation under limited conditions is useful, on the one hand, for measuring the achievement of the common economic purpose of the sales force—more effective sales—and, on the other hand, for evaluating the members of that organization in terms of their measurable contribution to that purpose, from (2) a standard of performance which, when applied to the concrete situation, also takes into account "organizational" and "personal" phenomena—interpersonal relations, social norms of behavior, hopes, fears. From this latter point of view the standard has to be thought of in relation to securing and maintaining the coöperation of particular people with particular personal situations who are in particular places in the organization.

The failure to keep these two aspects separate leads to much confusion and misunderstanding, and sometimes even to hurt feelings. Some administrators, for example, feel that using a "standard" interferes with, rather than assists in, the performance of their complex duties. It limits the exercise of their intuitive judgment of the complex concrete situation. It forces them sometimes into fudging the record. Some foremen, for example, will, in the case of an employee-rating plan, make the rating coincide more with what they want to be able to do in the future than with their impersonal judgment of the person's ability. They realize that if their rating does not coincide with what they do about a certain employee, then someone can raise a question: With such a high rating why have you not upgraded this man? How did you happen to make a supervisor of a man with such a low rating? Unable to explain satisfactorily to his superior why the rating does not coincide with his intuitive size-up of the complex situation, the foreman sees to it that he will not be put on the spot again.

Moreover, some of the specialists who devise these "controls" feel misunderstood. Many of them realize the limitations of their "logics" and do not want them misused. They want administrators to use them as convenient tools which will assist them but not completely solve their problems. Over and over again they urge them to use these partial logics "intelligently," "with common sense," "realistically."

At times the situation becomes serious. We find some teachers communicating these different specialist logics with a sort of ambivalence. They teach them as partial logics to be used "with a grain of salt." Inasmuch as the cerebral cortices of young students can more rapidly assimilate logics than a grain of salt, they leave their institutions of "learning" better skilled in handling logics than in handling human beings. Then discouragement faces them. Instead of finding their logics eagerly sought and welcomed by the business organizations to which they go, they discover that their first problem is to "sell" these logics to minor supervisors and employees who do not want them. But in their institutions of learning they were taught about "selling" in terms of "market analysis." They had not been instructed in how to sell logical ideas to people who prefer to behave nonlogically. Some of them come out of this bewilderment undamaged. By hook or by crook they finally get this grain of salt and go on to bigger and better things. Others never quite recover; they go on perfecting their logics on pieces of paper, far removed from the concrete territory to which they are to be ultimately applied.

What is Being Controlled?

The problem of the development of a skill would not be serious if all we were saying is that it requires wide experience as well as what can be learned from books. The change that occurs in a medical student after two years of internship could be cited as an example. But in our opinion the problem goes deeper than that. Maybe we can begin to see it more clearly if we compare medical education and business education as they exist today. In medicine not only the skills required but also the class of phenomena to which they relate, excluding for the moment those relating to mental illness, can be much more clearly formulated than they can in business. In medicine, as in business, a number of measuring devices exist which tell the physician something about the internal environment of his patient. However, no physician conceives that by measuring blood pressure or taking a basal metabolism he can cure his patient or influence his patient's behavior. Measurement assists him in making his diagnosis; it does not cure the patient. A number of laboratory technicians do not make up a medical practitioner.

A parallel can be drawn in business. These partial logics, of which we have spoken, help the administrator in diagnosing the situation. Only in this sense are they controls: they provide checks by means of which certain functions of the total enterprise can be evaluated in terms of the economic objective. For example, the figures of the cost accountant provide the administrator with a useful tool for diagnosing what may be wrong. The figures in themselves cannot cure the business. Cost control, quality control, production control, measuring the performance of workers, salesmen, foremen — all these are also diagnostic aids to the administrator. They do not in and by themselves do the administrator's job; they merely aid him in doing a better job in the same sense that a stethoscope and a thermometer assist the physician in making more adequate diagnoses. In other words, all these specialist logics do not make up an administrator.

But then the analogy breaks down, partly because of the more complex events and situations the administrator is trying to control. On the one hand, he is trying to control the attainment of the economic objective of the enterprise; on the other hand, he is trying to control concrete human behavior in the coöperative situation, which is the only means through which ultimately the common objective can be attained. This makes the administrator's problem exceedingly difficult. To try to use the same mechanism to achieve both kinds of control may be disastrous because the factors determining the attainment of the economic objective may not be of the same order and involve the same class of phenomena as those determining the coöperative situation. The physician in ordinary practice is sometimes up against the same problem, particularly when he has to secure the coöperation of the patient in following a treatment which involves a drastic change in his ways of life.

The class of phenomena with which the physician is dealing then ceases to be organic.

When measuring the performance of a worker, a salesman, or a foreman, what is being controlled? Does the measurement of a person's performance necessarily control or improve it? What is the connection between a standard in terms of which a person's performance can be measured and that person's performance? Putting the question in these forms, it is clear that a standard is merely one more factor in a person's environment to which he responds; and it is well to remember that his response may take different forms. If the standard has social sanction, it may operate on particular individuals with particular personal situations as an incentive to do better work. In our so-called competitive culture it is assumed that we all want to do better than our fellow men. Give us a standard and we break our necks trying to do better than the next person. But some of us do not react that way. A standard may also act as a deterrent to good work, as any experienced teacher knows. How often, as teachers, have we tried to tell our conscientious and worried students to forget about grades, that they are really not important, and with what results! In the eyes of some students, our function is to grade them, not teach them. As a result, how many academics finally come to accept the grading system as a necessary evil! How do we correct this situation? By keeping the grading system relatively simple and by adding to it occasionally a grain of salt? Or by trying to create bigger and better grading systems? There are tendencies in both directions, but let us not linger on this painful subject so near to home, but talk more in general.

Two Major Evaluational Systems in Business Organizations

It is well to remember that the items are infinite in terms of which people can be differentiated. People can be classified by the length of the nose, by the color of the eyes, by the kind of clothes they wear. Some of these classifications are more useful than others, depending upon the purpose for which the classification is to be used. In any informal social group, formal organization, or community, people are likely to be differentiated in terms of items expressing the social values of these social systems. Any noticeable similarity or difference in terms of age, sex, occupation, can become the basis of social classification. This process also goes on in business and industry. Employees, supervisors, and executives are being evaluated in terms of the tasks and duties they perform, in terms of the amount and the quality of work they do. They are also being evaluated by their fellow associates as contributors to group effort.

In any large business organization, there are at least two major evaluational systems in terms of which each contributor is being judged. In the case of one, he is evaluated in terms of certain measurable abstractions and standards relating to performance and efficiency. In the case of the other, he is being evaluated in terms of certain socially accepted codes and norms of conduct. The first evaluation tells him where he theoretically[6] stands in the eyes of management; the second tells him where he stands in the eyes of his fellow associates. These two evaluations of a person may not coincide. He may be judged a poor worker in terms of his output record, and he may be judged a "regular fellow" by his fellow workers. We do not mean to imply that these two evaluational systems always lead to opposing judgments, that is, that regular fellows are always "inefficient" and cannot be "efficient." The only implication is that the factors determining technical efficiency are not of the same order as those determining a regular fellow. In the second evaluation, coöperative phenomena cannot be conveniently ignored.

[6] The word "theoretically" is used here to imply that management people in practice are intuitively also taking into account other forms of evaluation.

There is no question that business organizations want regular fellows who are efficient. But how do they go about doing this? And what relation have their standards of performance to the formation and maintenance of regular fellows and efficient workers? It can be seen that these standards help in the direction of efficiency when the coöperative situation can be assumed as being satisfactory; that is, when it can be taken for granted that the individual and the group of which he is a member are working together as a team, that the standard is operating as an incentive, and that the supervisor applies the standard with "discretion" and "good judgment" in order to secure the coöperation of his group in attaining the economic objective. But what if the person is a member of a small group whose informal organization is at variance with the economic objective of the company? And what if the supervisor does not apply the standard with "discretion," "common sense," and "good judgment"? It is clear that in cases where the coöperative situation cannot be taken for granted the standard ceases to control behavior in the desired direction. In such a case, "control" can be exercised only by understanding the coöperative phenomena involved; and for this other skills are required.

WHAT SKILLS DOES THE ADMINISTRATOR USE IN DEALING WITH COÖPERATIVE PHENOMENA?

Let us summarize our discussion so far. In spite of the way our words may have sounded at times, we have not been advocating the return to a more primitive type of organization in business. We have not been saying, "Away with efficiency and all the gadgets it represents." We have not been depreciating their usefulness to business and the important contributions that they have made. We have not been implying that there is an inherent incompatibility between "efficiency" and "happiness."

What we have been trying to say is much simpler, namely,

that the factors which make for efficiency in a business organization are not necessarily the same as those factors that make for happiness, collaboration, teamwork, morale, or any other word which may be used to refer to coöperative situations. Two different sets of considerations are involved. In securing the first objective, under certain conditions certain useful abstractions from the total situation can be made and applied which take for granted the concrete coöperative situation. In attaining the second objective, coöperative phenomena are of the essence.

The problem is not a choice between two opposing alternatives — between "efficiency" on the one hand, and "morale" on the other; it is a problem of maintaining, under given conditions, a type and kind of equilibrium which will allow for maximum efficiency and collaboration. Now, this is the problem with which any administrator is confronted every day. He is trying to use every method which will cut costs, increase output, improve quality, cut down waste and accidents, and make his department or division technically efficient. At the same time, he is trying to secure the coöperation of individuals in attaining these technical ends. Not only does he have to secure their willingness to contribute their services to these purposes, but also he must see to it that by giving their services to these ends they will obtain social satisfactions which make them continuously desirous of coöperating. Now this is not a static problem of black and white. It is a dynamic problem of equilibrium; it is a problem of knowing the technological limitations, the limitations of the human organization, and the particular objectives that can be accomplished under these limiting conditions. In part, it is a problem of sizing up a situation and knowing what needs to be done and how it should be done here and now in order to attain the coöperative purpose. In part, it is the problem of a constant exercise of judgment in a situation of equilibrium, of assessing its nature, and of spotting possible sources of interference which may unduly disrupt the condition of balance.

To assist him in doing his job, the administrator has staff specialists or control agencies. Each of these specialists has specific functions. He selects from the total situation those aspects for which he is functionally responsible. Each is therefore evaluating the total situation in terms of the partial abstractions dictated by his specialty. Among these specialists in modern business must be included the personnel man. He too is responsible for certain functions: hiring, firing, placement, training, and welfare of employees. For each of these functions he too has specialized techniques: selection tests, job evaluation, employee-rating plans, conference techniques, pension plans, welfare plans.

Each of these specialists, control agencies, or functional staff groups can be arranged on a scale expressing the degree to which the application of its specialty involves coöperative phenomena. On one end would be the physicist, the chemist, the engineer. At the other end would be the rate setter, specialists engaged in job evaluation, measuring employee performance, and wage incentive systems. The latter groups are keenly aware of their relation to coöperative phenomena. They realize that their standards can be set only in coöperation with the different people and groups involved. At every turn the coöperation of employees, supervisors, and even top management must be sought. Only in this way can the desired results be achieved.

However, when the administrator has to conceive of his organization as a functioning whole and has to assess the contributions of each specialist group to it and make decisions in accordance with his size-up of the total situation, he is up against a concrete situation involving the interactions of people. And for this purpose what skills does he use? In terms of what data does he act? In what frame of reference is his thought set? If all the specialist skills are not the skill of the administrator, if all these partial controls of different specialist groups do not add up to the final control exercised by the administrator, then what is the administrative skill? What is that part of the situation which may be ignored or inaccurately stated by the limitations of a specialist logic, which must be understood and taken into account by the administrator if the control exercised is to be adequate? What, in short, does the administrator control?

CAN THE SKILLS THE ADMINISTRATOR USES IN DEALING WITH COÖPERATIVE PHENOMENA BE EXPLICITLY FORMULATED?

It is the thesis of this book that "good judgment," "long experience," "common sense," "discretion," "a grain of salt," "being realistic" are not sufficient answers to these questions. Granted that some people exercise these skills successfully, how do they do it? What is their point of view? How do they secure the coöperation of people? How does one conceive of a business organization as a functioning whole? What is the matrix from which can be made certain useful abstractions which ignore coöperative phenomena but which, when applied, have to take them into account?

It would be absurd to imagine that the answers to these questions are simple; nor is there any claim that they have been completely, finally, or definitively answered in the preceding chapters. Rather, in each chapter an attempt has been made to suggest more fruitful ways of stating certain problems involving coöperative phenomena and more profitable avenues of inquiry. It has been the intention to provoke research, and not more talk, on problems relating to coöperative phenomena.

Therefore, in no chapter have there been given, let us say, ten specific rules for securing collaboration, or ten things which a rate setter needs to take into account in order to get the coöperation of employees. These omissions were not unconsciously made in order to avoid being specific and practical.

Such rules and principles were deliberately omitted because in terms of the orientation which was suggested they are the height of impracticability. They substitute a verbal, ritualistic orientation for a diagnostic orientation to concrete situations. They try to solve a problem before they state it.

It is our attitude that "control" means understanding the nature of the phenomena with which one is dealing and the simple uniformities that can be found among them. This applies also to human control — the control of coöperative phenomena. This requires research, more research, continuous research, and research in which theory and practice go hand in hand. This, in our opinion, is the simple lesson to be learned from the history of the physical sciences. Man's control over his physical environment increased when he stopped trying to legislate verbally as to how and what the universe should be, and began to seek patiently and laboriously for the simple uniformities that existed in a limited class of data, and to behave, at least in respect to this aspect of his environment, in accordance with these uniformities.

It is our contention, therefore, that concrete events involving the interactions of people, which have been here referred to as "coöperative phenomena," constitute a class of phenomena which can be clearly segregated from other phenomena and can be studied for its own sake. This class of phenomena is a legitimate field of inquiry and research. For its study, a simple point of view can be formulated, simple methods can be developed, and simple uniformities can be observed, stated, and applied. In all these major aspects, it has the necessary characteristics of a legitimate discipline that can stand on its own feet and be studied for what it is worth.

CHAPTER IX

CONCERNING PEOPLE WHO THEORIZE ABOUT COÖPERATIVE PHENOMENA

IT IS a curious fact that those who deal with coöperative phenomena in business and those who theorize about them in universities, except for the economists, do not know each other very well. In this chapter, then, we shall attempt to introduce to businessmen some social scientists about whom they may never have heard but who we feel should not be completely ignored, in spite of the big words they use. Through this vicarious interaction it is hoped that some slight cross-fertilization of ideas with practice may occur.

About fifteen years ago, our Department posed two questions: (1) Who are the people outside of business who have studied, dealt with, and theorized about coöperative phenomena? (2) From them what can be learned in the form of fruitful working hypotheses, methods, or systematic knowledge which could be usefully applied in the industrial area for further study and investigation? For years, therefore, in conjunction with our field investigations, we have been trying to mobilize what social scientists could agree upon, in spite of verbal differences, as being valid. This turned out to be a much more difficult problem than was first anticipated.

CONCERNING THOSE WHO THEORIZE BUT DO NOT PRACTICE

In our journey through the field of social science, looking for what useful knowledge existed with regard to coöperative phenomena as the executive experiences them, we encountered one class of social scientists from whom we received little or no assistance. We shall give this class no title, for its members are legion and bear many different labels. Some have "chairs" in academic institutions; some do not. They all, however, have certain characteristics in common. Unlike the inarticulate men of action, they are people who are very articulate in discussing matters with which they sometimes have little firsthand acquaintance or experience. Some of them are "teachers," but they do not practice any skills, other than verbal ones, relating to social phenomena. They do not take into account the importance of the quality of judgment which is acquired by men of practical affairs. They hardly ever have the experience of making decisions and acting under the burden of responsibility. Hence, they indulge more freely in the kind of irresponsible talk and thinking so annoying to men of action.

These men are almost the polar opposite of the group we mentioned before — the men who practice but do not theorize about the skill they practice. Because of their difference in orientation — one to the concrete, the other to the verbal — they do not "get" each other. The verbalist tends to misjudge the man of action because the latter cannot verbalize what he intuitively knows and skillfully practices in the concrete situation. As a result, he thinks him a bore or "dumb." On the other hand, to the man of action the verbalist is an object of suspicion. How can a man talk so glibly about so many different things? How can he have opinions on so many different subjects? In defense, he dubs him a "theorist."

As a result, in the area of social science, more than in any other field, people are divided into two camps, the "theoretical" and the "practical." Each label becomes a fighting word for the other group. To call a man of affairs "theoretical," or its modern equivalents "New Dealer" or "brain truster," is to call forth from him a vehement denunciation, "What do you think I am? A so-and-so?" To call a man "practical" in some academic circles is almost to accuse him of being unscientific or unscholarly.

It is apparent that in this atmosphere of cordial distrust it has not been easy to introduce social theorists to men of practical affairs or vice versa. Inasmuch as each of the earlier chapters was originally a talk to businessmen, it was necessary to be sure that the theories presented were relevant to their practice, and, therefore, to distinguish those that were from those that were not.

One thing was clear: this group called "theorists" by men of action, without prejudging in any way their ultimate utility to society as a whole, were of no use to us. There were various reasons for this state of affairs: (1) They never thought in terms of the administrative context. (2) They never acted and made decisions under the burden of responsibility. (3) They were not interested in seeking simple uniformities in coöperative phenomena. Instead, (4) they preferred to indulge in large abstractions, noble sentiments, or great affairs. Hence, (5) their theories were not relevant to concrete practice. As a result, (6) they tended to seek political solutions; their talk abounded in "isms."

With the elimination of this group our problem was somewhat simplified, at least in numbers. It was clear that we had to seek theorists who were at the same time practicing a skill relating to the handling of concrete human situations — events involving the interactions of people. Their skill had to involve judgments in action and under the burden of responsibility. Their theories had to stand the test of observation and experiment — in other words, be demonstrated as useful and convenient ways of regarding the class of phenomena in question.

CONCERNING CERTAIN TENDENCIES WHICH DO NOT HELP MATTERS

These criteria helped in excluding certain tendencies which did not help to explain coöperative phenomena as the executive experiences them: (1) the tendency to keep social science pure and compartmentalized; (2) the tendency to study the individual either apart from his "social conditioning" or only in terms of it; (3) the tendency to consider verbal behavior either apart from the speaker's personal situation or only in terms of it; (4) the tendency to label people before trying to understand their situations.

The Tendency to Keep Social Science Pure and Compartmentalized

In trying to mobilize the existing knowledge regarding coöperative phenomena, it was evident that many different disciplines had contributed something to the subject. It was impossible to restrict ourselves to just one field. Studies relevant to this class of phenomena had been made by psychologists, sociologists, psychopathologists, social psychologists, human geographers, social anthropologists, psychoanalysts, social workers, to mention only a few of the many categories into which the theory and practice of social science can be subdivided. It might have been thought that all these different specialists would have provided a great deal of illumination on the subject, but instead the picture remained obscure and confused. Fierce battles raged among the different approaches and points of view. Nothing was quiet along this academic front.

It was difficult at times to see differentiations in the class of phenomena to which these different specializations related. Some of the distinctions seemed arbitrary. If one studied the culture of a primitive group, for example, one was an "anthropologist." If one studied fringe groups in our present industrial culture, one was a "sociologist." If one studied the relations between producers and consumers in our present culture, one was an "economist." If one studied the universal responses of human beings regardless of their culture (or rats, preferably), one was a "psychologist." And then some "psychologists" found it difficult to differentiate themselves from "physiologists."

If one allowed another person to talk to him informally for an hour, one was perhaps a "friend" or an "educator"; formally, for one to three hours, with a questionnaire to boot, a "vocational guider," a "public opinion poller," or a "social psychologist"; for two to three hours, with true-and-false tests thrown in, a "psychometrist"; for two years without interruption, a "psychoanalyst." Of course, if in the process one could compute a standard deviation for these verbal responses, one was "scientific."

If one studied the responses of children in the schoolroom situation, one was studying "learning" or "intelligence" — one was an "educational psychologist" or "child psychologist" perhaps. If one studied the responses of workers on the job, one was studying "fatigue" or "monetary incentive" — one was an "industrial psychologist." If one studied the responses of a harassed person not doing well in his job, or perhaps "out of a job," and possibly in a "mental hospital," one was studying "frustrations" and "aggressions" — one was perhaps an "abnormal psychologist," a "psychopathologist," a "psychoanalyst," a "neuropsychologist," a "psychoneurologist," an "orthopsychiatrist," or a "mental hygienist," to mention only a few of the labels which might be applied. Of course, the more one could study the responses of a person under conditions as completely different as possible from those he usually enjoyed — so-called "experimental" conditions — the more "scientific" one became.

We began to understand better why there existed this hiatus between social scientists, on the one hand, and people who were trying to practice coöperation in business, on the other. With the verbal battles raging among social scientists themselves, with the many different schools of thought, with the many different points of view and theories regarding human motivation, with each school of thought bearing a different label — how could the administrator (a practicing social scientist, although he did not know it) choose among them? Quite rightly, he ignored them and went about his own business while they settled their own personal quarrels.

Were the situation not deplorable, it would be comic. On the one hand, we found in business and industry people who were actually practicing a skill of handling coöperative phenomena receiving almost no aid from — in fact, hardly being on speaking terms with — those who might have been expected to contribute valuable theories about this class of phenomena. On the other hand, we found sociologists flocking to study people before they entered or after they left the economic structure: in schools, recreational groups, mental hospitals, clinics, family welfare associations, prisons. The anthropologists studied the sex life, habits, customs, and rituals of primitive groups far removed from our industrial civilization.

Meanwhile, within our economic organizations there was allowed to flourish a conception of human motivation — of little economic men and little economic women, each motivated by his or her economic interest — so bizarre and so fantastic that it made the myths of primitive people pale by comparison. For a time it looked as if only children, primitive people, and the "insane" were allowed to have sex lives, complexes, habits, customs, day and night dreams, preoccupations, and other manifestations of the nonlogical. In business and industry, administrators, executives, and employees seemed to have only cerebral cortices. Their behavior, in every respect, was logical. They never indulged in wishful thinking. Even at the level of collective bargaining, they were manifesting only the purely logical interest of economic gain.

As a result, we had two social sciences standing side by side with no interpenetration: "economics" was concerned with the logical behavior of administrators, executives, employees, and consumers; "sociology" was concerned with the behavior of immigrants, delinquents, the unemployed, the mentally deranged, and the child.

The Tendency to Consider the Individual Apart from His "Social Conditioning" or only in Terms of It

In practice one is dealing with concrete, particular people; one is not handling Thought or Behavior in general. In business, for example, the executive is not dealing with human nature in general; he is handling Tom, Dick, and Harry. The knowledge he needs is a knowledge of the situations of Tom, Dick, and Harry which will help him to handle them better. In this sense, the administrator is in a clinical setting, not an experimental setting. Therefore, it gives the administrator little help in handling Tom to know that "self-preservation is the first law of nature," particularly when Tom, who may be harassed and worried about his personal situation, threatens to commit suicide.

From the point of view of utility then, if nothing else, little help is obtained from those fields of specialization which tend to treat the individual here and now apart from his social conditioning. In fact, the generalizations derived from such studies succeed fairly well in excluding the very class of phenomena with which the executive has to deal in handling coöperative situations. Moreover, the behavior of an organism apart from its social conditioning is well treated and considered by physiology. Here can be studied fruitfully those changes in the internal environment of the person (chemical constituents of the blood, etc.) which accompany certain physical changes in the external environment (high or low temperatures, high altitudes, severe exercise, etc.). The remainder of the problem, with which, quite rightly, the physiologist is not concerned—it is outside of the limited class of phenomena with which his specialization deals—involves responses to words and stimuli containing "meaning." A simple example may suffice to make this distinction clear: If Cow 1 kicks Cow 2, Cow 2 may receive a broken leg; but "meaning" is not seriously involved. However, if Smith 1 kicks Smith 2, and Smith 1 is an American and Smith 2 is a German, "meaning" is involved. From such a simple interaction, more may result and more is involved than Smith 2's broken leg.

It seemed to us, therefore, useful to keep two classes of phenomena separate: (1) those events in which meaning can be completely ignored or conveniently ignored for certain purposes; (2) those events in which meaning cannot be conveniently ignored. Surely the everyday affairs of an executive are mostly concerned with this second class of phenomena, that is, responses to words and stimuli involving meaning. Moreover, the meanings people assign to their everyday experiences are not entirely or always "logical." They involve sentiments, and the sentiments are in part related to the personal history and present social situation of the person. Therefore, any field of study which attempted to study the responses of a person apart from meaning, and meaning apart from social context, seemed to us to be of little value for the everyday world of the busy executive.

In reaction to this tendency to treat the individual apart from his social milieu there was among some social scientists a swing in the opposite direction. The individual was conceived of merely as a resultant of his early "social conditioning." For a time, it looked as if man had only simple and conditioned reflexes. He was treated as if he were devoid of any present skills, logical or social, whereby he might adapt himself to his environment. He was just a piece of pulsating protoplasm, conditioned for ever and ever to this particular eccentricity of behavior because of some early traumatic or other unfortunate experience. Everything was "conditioned," not "conditional" or "capable of reconditioning."

In some cases this point of view is useful. In certain personal situations, it can be conjectured that a person's basic attitudes and responses have been determined by his early childhood experiences. The person's relation to the socio-reality about him can be viewed as an extension of the early familial configuration. One can see how he is relating himself to his adult surroundings in terms of preoccupations conditioned by the early family situation which persist long after the childhood situation ceases to exist in fact. Therefore, a careful examination of these earlier events, as well as the meanings attaching to them, in order to find out how the distortion of attitude was slowly built up, not only provides much insight but also helps the individual to modify his attitudes.

The deficiency of this point of view, however, for daily administrative practice, is apparent to anyone who has lived in the administrative milieu. It is considering the characteristics of personal behavior outside of coöperative systems. It is primarily the study of people who have been living in a social void—people who are unfitted for coöperation, or at least, because of their early conditioning, have not been prepared for coöperation. It is primarily the study of people through one set of relations (familial) to the neglect of all others (social structures or formal organizations in which man participates). As a study limited to those factors in the conditioning of a person which have unfitted him for coöperation, it is highly useful. As a generalized point of view with regard to man's behavior in coöperative systems, however, it remains inadequate. For the administrator, who is primarily dealing with people in coöperative systems, it is therefore insufficient.

The conception of a person as merely a resultant of his social conditioning reduces man to "wishes," "frustrations," "aggressions," and so on. On this side it provides a useful picture. We see more clearly those factors which a person is bringing to the situation—the demands he is making of it and the expectations he has of it. What remains obscure from this point of view is that to which the person is relating himself—that to which he is bringing his hopes and fears and expectations. As a result, a one-sided picture is obtained. We understand better the demands the person is making of the situation; we do not understand as well the demands the situation is making of the person.

The Tendency to Consider Verbal Behavior Apart from the Personal Situation of the Speaker or only in Terms of It

It is perhaps a commonplace to say that coöperative phenomena include verbal data and that a good bit of the administrator's environment is verbal. Not only does he use words to inform and persuade; he is constantly listening to people who are trying to tell him of their purposes and to affect his feelings. What contribution has social science made to the problem of interpreting what people say?

Three modern schools of thought have thrown considerable light on this question: psychoanalysis, functional anthropology, and semantics. It would be absurd, in the limited space of this chapter, to try to state their contributions and to give them the serious attention they deserve. There is little question that, in general, social science has given too little consideration to this most important aspect of coöperative phenomena.

Experience shows that language is not only used for purposes of making informative, factual, or logical statements; it is also used to express sentiments and feelings. This is a simple proposition which anyone can confirm in terms of his own experience, and yet it does not seem to be very well understood. To us, it has seemed useful and convenient to keep clear and distinct two different kinds of statements: (1) those which are approximately verifiable by experience, observation, and experiment; (2) those in which verifiability is not in question because they are not statements of fact—their function is not to communicate information but to express feeling.

To confuse these two classes of statements is serious. To ask of statements of the second class that they conform to the properties of the first is absurd, just as absurd as to ask a dog to have the characteristics of a cat or to evaluate a dog's behavior in terms of the way a cat would behave. And yet this is what frequently happens. Statements of the second class are constantly being made—as, for example, "Woman's place is in the home"—and they are treated as if they were statements of the first class. As a result, there are verbal arguments and bitter feelings.

It is our contention that statements of the second class have no meaning apart from their personal and social context. They refer to the personal and social life of the speaker. Therefore it is well to regard such statements in terms of his total situation. Inasmuch as man in his daily life indulges far more in statements of the second class than in those of the first, it is likely that with this orientation toward what people say one will commit fewer errors than by treating everything said as either fact or error. On the other hand, this orientation can be carried to excess.

When some of us (particularly those who have been shut up most of our lives in libraries and have not interacted very much with our fellow men, except through books) first make this discovery about language—that man makes noises to express pleasure and pain, to amuse himself, for the sake of making a noise, to affirm his solidarity with social groups in which he participates, and sometimes "unconsciously" to express his innermost feelings, desires, and longings—we are blinded by the illumination it brings. For a time the world is bifurcated into (1) the world of books pertaining to matters of fact and logic; and (2) the mundane world outside of libraries, where man expresses feelings and sentiments and makes noises for the sake of making noises. Then a gnawing doubt begins. Perhaps also in the world of books men are making noises just for the sake of making noises and to express sentiments relating to frustrations. Perhaps we are also in the same uncomfortable boat. And then the world comes tumbling down around our ears.

Now it is during this period of disintegration that our initial illumination can be carried too far. Everything becomes symptomatic of some inner frustration, secret wish, or dark mystery. The slightest gesture or slip of the tongue is eagerly pounced upon as being indicative of something which happened long ago in the speaker's early childhood. Inasmuch as that to which the manifest statement refers is "unconscious" to the speaker but, in some way, as clear as crystal to the listening social scientist, a merry time is had by the latter. Nobody's life remains private. The simplest statement reveals all. In some circles it even becomes popular to refute anything a person says by affirming, "Well, of course, he is merely compensating aggressively for such and such a frustration."

Now this personal diagnosis may explain some statements a person makes, but he may make certain other statements to which it has no reference. It is well to remember that people often make statements whose truth or falsity does not depend upon their personal histories. Then, in fact, the personal consideration is irrelevant and meaningless. There are statements which are verifiable, and when such a statement is made, only the tests of experience, observation, and experiment apply. Even an abnormal person may make statements of this class. Not all remarks made by "insane" people are insane. Likewise, not all remarks made by "sane" people are logical or factual. In the written or spoken word, therefore, it is well to separate statements of fact from those in which sentiments are being expressed. To the former the private life of the author is irrelevant, and only the tests of observation and experience apply. To the latter the categories of fact and error are irrelevant; only the personal and social situation of the speaker applies.

The Tendency to Label People before Trying to Diagnose Their Situations

The executive has to size up human beings and human situations. In this respect, his orientation is like that of the clinician. He has to make diagnoses. Many times he has to handle a situation which is unsatisfactory to some one or more individuals. Inasmuch as often the source of the discontent cannot be accurately stated by the complainant, it is up to him to go from the symptoms to the underlying situation. Although he realizes that each individual is unique and is bringing to the work situation a different background and a different set of personal experiences, he is also aware when handling any one person that what he does may affect that person's relations with other persons in the organization. In his decisions with regard to Tom, for example, he has to think of Tom's relation to Bill and the possible effect on Bill of any proposed action on Tom. This is the organizational side of the administrator's problem. He is dealing not only with Tom as an individual, but also with Tom as a member of an organization or a group. His diagnoses, therefore, have to be organizational diagnoses as well as individual. Probably no more difficult diagnoses have to be made.

To the understanding of this complex situation the social scientist has brought little help. To the administrator the classificatory systems into which personalities can be divided are very seldom of more help than the intuitive judgments made by people in the situation, and sometimes not even as much. The tendency is to label rather than diagnose. Each person is put into his or her little cubby-hole and viewed statically as a member of that particular classification. This point of view leads to the search for square pegs for square holes and round pegs for round holes. It misses the dynamic interrelations between a person and his environment. Instead of asking, "What is this person's situation?" one substitutes a label, and the person's situation is conceived of as being completely exhausted or explained by the assigning of the label. Frequently this tendency can degenerate into a kind of witch hunt. For some reason interesting to note, most of the classifications are two-valued. One of the names tends to be "bad" or "undesirable." As a result, more often than not these classificatory systems are used as a means of excluding certain people bearing the wrong label from participating in coöperative activities. For them there are no holes, either round or square.

This is not a condemnation of classification in general. Classification is useful, important, and a necessary first step in the attainment of systematic knowledge. For those who realize that the labels we give to things and where we draw the line between one class of things and another depend upon our interests and the purposes of our classification, little difficulty arises. When classification is so regarded, there is no question of its convenience and utility. But when we think that because there exists a name there is one thing in fact to which it refers, or when we think that because we have a class name the concrete behavior of a person can be completely exhausted or explained by it, very serious results can follow, particularly for the person being classified.[1]

This situation is still further complicated by the fact that, although those who originate these classifications may be quite aware of their limitations, those who use them may not be, as anyone can observe by seeing the glib way in which terms

[1] This may be the appropriate place to explain the frequent and perhaps annoying use of quotation marks. Their purpose in most cases has been to guard the reader from making this very error. They have been saying: Remember that the classes and the names given to them have been made for certain purposes by the author. It is hoped that some of the distinctions will be found useful or convenient. Do not search for some inner mysterious meaning.

such as "introvert," "extrovert," "inferiority complex" are bandied about.

CONCERNING THE NEED FOR A CONCEPT OF A "SOCIAL SYSTEM"

But, more important still, most of these classifications are classifying individuals rather than dynamic situations involving the interactions of people. As a result, they tend to exclude coöperative phenomena; they fail to catch the condition of interdependence which obtains among the phenomena with which the executive has to deal. For this complexity in the territory a simple cause-and-effect analysis of the situation is substituted. The names or labels applied to a person are treated as simple causes of the person's behavior. Such an orientation encourages the "fallacy of misplaced concreteness." As a result, instead of discouraging one of the principal sources of error in the thinking of the layman with regard to social phenomena, through these oversimplified classifications "science" assists in the process.

No conceptual framework can do more violence to the territory of the executive, or of anyone who is dealing concretely with coöperative phenomena, than this simple notion of cause and effect. For such a person in a position of responsibility a concept of a system involving relations of interdependence is much more useful because it structurally represents the complex events and their interrelations with which he has to deal.

CHAPTER X

MANAGEMENT AND MORALE

CONCERNING THE PRACTICE OF SOME SOCIAL SCIENTISTS

IN THE preceding chapter we have been concerned with theories which fail to represent coöperative phenomena as the executive intuitively experiences them. This criticism cannot be made of all generalizations in the field of social science. Some of them have been developed in relation to practice and in a context comparable to that of the administrator. The clinician, whether he be psychiatrist, psychologist, psychopathologist, psychoanalyst, or child psychologist, when he has been concerned with helping people to adjust more effectively to their environment, has had to deal with and theorize about coöperative phenomena in a position of responsibility. The sociologist, the social anthropologist in his field investigations of communities, the social case worker, the penologist have been in similar positions.

From them a great deal of empirical knowledge has been gained. Among them exists a common fund of knowledge acquired from dealing with essentially the same class of phenomena; and yet, curiously enough, this common knowledge has remained, just as in the case of the administrator, much on an intuitive level. In these fields we can find, just as we did in the case of the administrator, the skillful clinician who does a good job with little theory and sometimes even in spite of the theories he holds. We also find those who can expound with great ease and clarity the theories of Freud and yet would be stumped if presented with a concrete case of psychoneurosis to handle.

It is our opinion that this common element underlying the

practice of these different specializations has been disguised because of the tremendous emphasis on differences in theory. That which in terms of theory has been separating them has in terms of practice been pulling them together, so that, coincident with the tendency to separate into different schools of thought in terms of theory, there has been an equally strong tendency on the part of those more concerned with practice to come together and pool their common fund of knowledge and experience.

From the point of view of practice, the arbitrariness of some of the distinctions has been only too evident. Only those whose orientation to words and labels is so strong as to make the orientation to situations impossible could fail to see, for example, the similarity in context which exists in certain important respects for the administrator handling a dissatisfied employee, for the psychiatrist handling a mild case of obsession, or for the social worker handling a client. Granted that there are also important differences among these three situations which should be kept in mind, there are certain simple generalizations which apply to the effective handling of all of them.

It seems absurd to think that in dealing with such common phenomena the administrator should think about the human being in one way, the psychiatrist in another way, and the social worker in still another — that each should have different theories with regard to human motivation and behavior. There is no wide and sharp split of orientation between the practice of the garage mechanic and the practice of the engineer or the physicist. We do not find garage mechanics trying to exorcise devils out of the hoods of automobiles — a class of phenomena with which the physicist or engineer is not concerned. Why then should there be this sharp and wide split of orientation between the administrator, the psychiatrist, and the sociologist, when each is dealing with essentially the same limited class of phenomena? If in fact it does not exist in skillful practice, why does it exist in theory?

It will be the purpose, therefore, of this chapter to make a few simple statements with regard to what seems to us to be the general common orientation in point of view and method which exists among all these different specializations, when it comes down to the responsible practice of them in dealing with that limited class of phenomena we have called "coöperative." In our opinion, the essential groundwork of collecting facts and the systematic search for simple uniformities among them in a wide variety of situations have not as yet gone very far. A few simple steps have been taken in this direction, and each step has more than confirmed our expectations; but more research is needed. What is said here can be only tentative and suggestive. As we have said before, our hope is to stimulate more research and less talk about matters of human collaboration. To talk very much about a knowledge which exists, if at all, in only an embryonic stage puts one into an uncomfortable position. We shall try to set a good example by being brief.

CONCERNING THE CONTROL OF COÖPERATIVE PHENOMENA

Probably the simplest statement we have made, perhaps only by suggestion, is that practice occurs in the present and not in the future. We cannot practice in the future; we can only practice *here and now*. If, therefore, we are to control future events, particularly events involving the interactions of persons, we must do something here and now which will have the desired consequences. When effective control is to be exercised by the executive, it has to be exercised at the point of action in the present.

Therefore, the kind of knowledge which tells an executive what a desirable state of affairs in his human organization should be is not so helpful as statements regarding the immediate steps he should take in order to reach this end. It is one thing to tell him that the "morale" of his organization is not very high; it is another thing to know what to do here and now in order to improve it.

We have met this problem before. A person's performance can be measured in terms of a standard. But in what sense is his behavior controlled? The standard can tell how much a person's performance falls short of what is expected of him; it may determine whether or not a person is allowed to stay on the job. This is one kind of "control" which the executive can exercise. Under certain conditions the standard may control the person's future performance; that is, his performance may improve. This is another kind of "control." But whether it improves or not, the standard says absolutely nothing with regard to why here and now the person's performance falls short of what is expected of him and what can be done here and now to improve it. This is a third kind of "control."

This last kind of control can be exercised only through a diagnosis of the human situation. It depends upon a diagnosis of the present factors limiting the person's performance. It means operating here and now upon these limiting factors. When an administrator is in this orientation, he is acting very much like a physician or an engineer, although he is dealing with another class of phenomena. He is exercising "human control" by a knowledge of the uniformities among relations existing in the situation here and now, and he is acting here and now in terms of these uniformities.

There is another type of human control the executive can exercise which in some respects may be very similar, but in other respects very different. Any person who is in a position of responsibility in a business organization may exercise human control by using words or stimuli of one kind or another to impose certain standards of behavior. In this way he hopes to bring about certain future events. Much of our language has this function—through words we attempt to direct, influence, control the future actions of our fellow men.[1]

Generally the language we use for this purpose is anything but matter of fact; it is likely to be full of feeling and emotion. Perhaps it is for this reason that we fail to note that the "standards" in terms of which we measure the performance of a person may have exactly the same function. They are "controls" only in the sense that they influence the future action of people by imposing patterns of behavior. In this sense, the difference between the old-fashioned supervisor who exercised control by saying, "Bill, get the lead out of your pants," and the modern supervisor who exercises control by pointing out to Bill his performance in relation to a standard is only one of degree. To the extent that the old-fashioned supervisor may have known Bill and his situation and addressed his remark to that context, while the modern supervisor may be addressing his standard to an undifferentiated worker, the former may have an edge on the latter. In either case, the explicit understanding of the human situation is lacking.

This example may help to distinguish the two different kinds of control. In one case we may try to influence a person's behavior by using words which are addressed to that person's situation. We hope that they will have the desired effect because they are utterances with collective sanction in the group of which the person is a member, or they are appealing to that person's most fundamental residues of behavior. In the other case we may use the same words without effect because they are not being addressed to that particular situation. The first kind of control, if done either explicitly or intuitively, does not differ very much from the kind of control we previously mentioned — a control which is dependent upon a knowledge of the uniformities among relations existing here and now in the situation. The second kind of control is quite different.

[1] For an interesting discussion of this point, see S. I. Hayakawa, *Language in Action* (Chicago: Institute of General Semantics, 1940).

It becomes a sort of verbal magic — a kind of control which has long since disappeared in the exact sciences — an attempt to control future events by magical words rather than by an understanding of situations.

In the case of our previous example, the supervisor who says to Bill, "Get the lead out of your pants," with an explicit knowledge of or at least an acquaintance with Bill and his situation and the collective sentiments and beliefs of the group of which Bill is a member, may be acting very effectively. Without such knowledge, however, the hope that in all cases all workers can be motivated by the phrase, "Get the lead out of your pants," is futile. The same point can be made about standards. Standards, too, can constitute effective human control or can be nothing more than exercises in verbal magic. Whether they are one or the other depends upon the way they are being used and a knowledge of the situation to which they are being applied. But how is this knowledge of human situations acquired?

What "Psychopathologists" have had to Say about the Control of Coöperative Phenomena

Modern psychopathology has contributed a great deal to the subject of "control." According to this school of thought, man has roughly two ways of controlling his environment: (1) by trying to change his environment to conform to his wishes, and (2) by modifying his wishes and expectations to fit in with his environment. Whichever form this control takes in a particular situation, the better part of wisdom is to control those things over which one can have some control and not to try to control those things over which one can have little or no control. For example, if a person is worried about what his fellow associates think of him, it is sometimes better for him to try to control his preoccupation that he is not liked by his fellow associates — something over which he can learn to exercise some control — rather than to go around frantically trying to get his fellow associates to like him, that is, trying to control the likes and dislikes of other people — something over which he has no control. On the other hand, if a person is afraid of being run over by a train and he happens to be standing on a railroad track and hears a train approaching, it is wiser for him to control the situation by jumping off the track than to try to control his fear.

"Control" in this sense implies knowing something about the class of phenomena to which the control is to be applied in a given situation. Psychopathology has shown that people who have difficulty in getting along with their fellow men, or who, for one reason or another, are nervous, harassed, timid, or apprehensive, can be helped by a minute exploration of their situations in order to determine those factors here and now which are tending to produce these symptoms and difficulties. In this connection it should be remembered that many things which happened years ago can operate here and now in the form of interfering preoccupations.

Now this implies a new conception of human control. It implies a control through an understanding of situations. By such understanding a person can gradually find out what he needs to do as well as what he can do here and now to make matters better for himself. He may, for example, learn that he should seek more the association of other people and learn how to live and work better with his fellow men. He may try to do something in this direction and painfully and slowly acquire new social skills of relating himself to his fellow men — skills with which his early family situation and later educational development had failed to provide him. He may find, at the same time, that he also needs to change certain maps inside his head which are inaccurately representing the kind of world in which he lives. This is another class of phenomena. He may find that some of his trouble comes from the fact that he is trying to make the world conform to these peculiar maps inside his head rather than trying to make these maps conform to the kind of world in which he lives. In this process of acquiring insight, his expectations may become modified. Instead of asking the world to conform entirely to his wishes, he learns how to relate himself to the world in which he lives. Between these two tendencies, he learns to achieve a comfortable working equilibrium.

Now many people who are skillfully helping others in this fashion — regardless of the labels they may bear, the different ways in which they may state the techniques they practice, and the different theories they may profess — are expressing in practice a very similar orientation. It is an orientation which addresses itself to the concrete situation. The control they exercise is achieved through understanding how a person got that way before recommending a cure. It pays attention to limiting conditions as well as to the strategic factors in the present situation about which something can be done. In many cases of personal maladjustment, the structure of the thinking here and now may be the most important factor; and it is often the thing about which something not only should be but can be done.

What "Sociologists" and "Social Anthropologists" have had to Say about the Control of Coöperative Phenomena

Sociologists and social anthropologists have also thrown considerable illumination on the problem of control. According to this school of thought, man from the date of birth lives in a social milieu. This social milieu is not a mere aggregate of individuals; it is an ordered set of conditions which has a character. In short, man is born into a specific family group which has certain ways of life, certain codes of behavior. It is related in certain ways to other families in the community. It has a certain cultural background. The process of educating the new member who is born into a specific family group is to transmit the existing culture to him. It is preparing him for social life — for increasingly wider social participation. In this process not only the immediate family group, but the school and the church also play their parts. The early meanings a person assigns to his experience are largely in terms of these codes of behavior and associated beliefs. As the child grows up and participates in groups other than the immediate family, he loses more and more of his egocentricity. He learns to achieve more adequate social skills of relating himself to his social environment.

This point of view suggests that these cultural patterns of behavior, this vast network of customary ways of doing things into which we are born, constitute the chief control on our lives. Only by such codes is behavior predictable or coöperation possible. Only through them can social control be exercised. Without them there would be no such thing as society. In order to exist, society must impose patterns of behavior on its members. It must make husbands dutiful to their wives, children obedient to their parents.

Now any administrator or person responsible for the work of others intuitively recognizes that much effective collaboration among people is dependent upon conforming to certain codes of behavior without any conscious process of deciding whether one will or will not coöperate. A standard with collective sanction for the group to which it is applied is easier to administer than a standard without such sanction, for without such sanction the standard can be maintained only by force. Without accepted codes of behavior the spontaneity of collaboration is lost. Although this is intuitively understood by the skillful practitioner of human relations, it is far from being explicitly recognized in the partial logics of management by means of which "control" is also exercised.

CONCERNING THE DIAGNOSIS OF COÖPERATIVE PHENOMENA

Our point up to now has been that effective human control can be exercised by a person in a position of responsibility only through an adequate understanding of the human situations he is administering. He has to know something about the individuals under his charge; he has to know something about their social as well as technical organization. He has to be alert to changes which may be occurring in either or both of these areas and their possible effects on the total situation; for example, what effects in his organization may result from a rapid introduction of new employees or of new techniques. All this requires a capacity on his part to diagnose the individual and group situations under his charge. For this purpose he uses certain intuitive skills. But can these skills be more clearly formulated?

If these skills are capable of being made explicit and of being taught, they involve, as we have stated before: (1) a clear understanding of the limited class of phenomena to which they are addressed, (2) a useful way of thinking about this class of phenomena, and (3) simple methods for obtaining the data. We have had much to say about understanding the limited class of phenomena with which these skills are concerned. We have tried to demonstrate that coöperative phenomena are capable of being clearly differentiated from other classes of phenomena and of constituting a legitimate field of inquiry. We shall now consider the other two requirements.

Concerning a Useful Way of Thinking about Coöperative Phenomena

By indirection, we have been suggesting a concept of equilibrium as a useful way of regarding the complex interactions of people in a coöperative system. It is a way of thinking which, if followed, prevents us from making a simple cause-and-effect analysis of phenomena in which a relation of interdependence obtains. We have been suggesting the concept of a social system in which the components of the system are individuals having certain properties as well as certain relations to one another. "The properties and relations of persons exist not in a changeless state, but in a state of flux. However, the instantaneous states and the changes are not chaotic or random states and changes. On the contrary, they are in general subject to connections and constraints of a kind that may be referred to, or considered as in a measure determined by, the condition of equilibrium . . . defined by Pareto as 'a state such that if a small [not too great] modification different from that which will otherwise occur is impressed upon a system, a reaction will at once appear tending toward the conditions that would have existed if the modification had not been impressed.' "[2]

In Part I, we have been giving popular expression to this point of view. We have been suggesting that in a business organization some of the important properties and relations of the components of the system are:

(1) the "social conditioning" of the individuals who go to make up the organization — what they are bringing to the situation in terms of (a) social codes of behavior, collective beliefs, and sentiments, (b) personal skills, (c) asocial attitudes — obsessive and irrational preoccupations, (d) economic interests, and (e) logical skills;

(2) the formal patterns of behavior of the organization, with their associated sentiments and beliefs, to which the individual has to conform and which are prescribed by the rules, regulations, and policies of the company — which we shall generally refer to as "formal organization";

[2] L. J. Henderson, *Three Lectures on Concrete Sociology*, p. 21.

(3) the informal patterns of behavior of particular work groups, with their associated sentiments and beliefs, to which the individual also has to conform, i.e. the particular codes and routines of behavior of local groups — which we shall refer to as "informal organization."

We can conceive of these parts as so interrelated and interdependent that any change in one part of the social system will be accompanied by changes in other parts of the system. There is a disparity in the rates of change possible in different parts of the system. The formal organization can change more rapidly than the informal; the informal organization can change more rapidly than the social conditioning of the individuals who go to make up informal work groups. In this disparity in the rates of change we shall look for conditions of unbalance which may manifest themselves in different forms.[8]

It is our contention that this condition of equilibrium is that to which the skillful administrator is addressing himself when handling coöperative phenomena. It is through his understanding of this condition of equilibrium, and the possible sources of interference which may produce an unbalance, that he exercises "control." It is only through his knowledge of the factors making for or against the condition of equilibrium that he can do something here and now. It is a control of the future by an understanding of the conditions determining the present state of equilibrium rather than an attempt to produce

[8] It is not our intention here to give a systematic statement of this way of regarding coöperative phenomena. For those who are interested in a more systematic statement as applied to the human problems of a business organization, see Roethlisberger and Dickson, *Management and the Worker* (Cambridge: Harvard University Press, 1939), chapters xxiv–xxvi. See also Chester I. Barnard, *The Functions of the Executive.* For a more general statement of the concept of a social system, see L. J. Henderson, *Three Lectures on Concrete Sociology.* The author has made considerable use of both of these latter statements in preparing this chapter.

future event *B* by putting into effect event *A* with the hope that cause *A* will produce effect *B* regardless of the situation of equilibrium that obtains.

This is the administrative context in which men of action who are responsible for the actions of others often find themselves. From the point of view of the nervous system it is not a comfortable position in which to be. It is often difficult to produce a desirable state of affairs *B* under the present conditions of equilibrium *A*, for the factors determining equilibrium *A* may be such as to allow *B* to be achieved only by introducing undesirable factors *C*, *D*, and *E*. It is little wonder that men who daily live in this context are often rendered speechless and feel they are misunderstood by social reformers, social planners, and social theorists. Dreams of Utopia have little place in their lives. It is their function to keep the world steady for others, that is, to maintain that condition of equilibrium which makes for feelings of security and "morale" in their organizations.

Concerning Simple Methods of Obtaining the Data

Both psychopathology and sociology have contributed useful methods to the study and diagnosis of individual and group situations. One may be called "the interviewing method"; the other may be called "the method of social observation." Through the combined use of both methods, in any human situation in a business organization one can learn what is important to people—their hopes and fears, what may be interfering with their work, what may be the sources of their dissatisfactions and difficulties, to what groups they belong, the extent and nature of their participation, their positions in informal groups, as well as the effect that technical changes, management logics, and methods of supervision may have on these factors. As a result, a human diagnosis of the concrete situation can be made, in terms of which something can be done here and now, if need be, to improve the coöperative situation.[4]

It may be well here to consider the extent to which the administrator himself should or can practice these skills of diagnosing human situations. Although from a certain aspect this is an important consideration, we have not dealt with this problem anywhere in this book. Our position is very simple and brief. It seems to us of first importance, at this stage of our development, to state the conditions and limits of the skills, the limited class of phenomena to which they can be applied and practiced usefully under certain given conditions. This has been the level at which this book has been written. It has been affirming two propositions: (1) these skills can be clearly formulated, can be made communicable, and can be usefully applied; (2) business organizations, particularly large ones, need them. It therefore seemed of secondary importance to try to state how these skills can or should be introduced in a business organization and by whom they should be applied — by the line administrator or a staff specialist. In fact, to say anything on this matter is either talking out of turn and trying to control things over which we have no control, or trying to dictate to whom knowledge should be made available.

In terms of the limited experience we have had so far, it is our opinion that these skills can be practiced at different levels. It seems to us common sense that there should be no cleavage in orientation or point of view with regard to thinking about coöperative phenomena among the different people in positions of responsibility in a business organization who deal with such phenomena. But with the systematic daily application of these skills to concrete situations, a number of peculiar considerations come in which will vary from one organization to an-

[4] For a more systematic treatment of interviewing and observation as applied to the human problems of a business organization, see Roethlisberger and Dickson, *Management and the Worker*, chapter xiii and Part IV.

other. It is perhaps needless to say that these skills cannot be learned overnight and that they have to be practiced in order that persons should become proficient in their use.

MANAGEMENT AND MORALE

It may be surprising to some that the word "morale" has appeared so infrequently in a chapter on the subject. This has been done intentionally to avoid thinking about a vague word. Rather, the intention has been to think about more concrete phenomena to which, if it is to have any meaning, the word "morale" can now be referred.

For any person who has held a position of responsibility in a business organization—or any organization for that matter—the word "morale" comes to have real meaning; that is, it refers to something which is felt to be of great importance, even if that something remains vague and illusive. It pertains to the relations of individuals in a group or larger organization, rather than to the individual alone. To talk of the "morale" of an individual, apart from the group or organization to which he contributes his services, is to talk about personal characteristics of behavior outside of coöperative systems. Individuals can be so characterized. It will be remembered that we did mention certain individuals who because of their past social experiences were unfitted for coöperation. In this sense it is well to remember that the social conditioning of the individuals who make up an organization may constitute an important factor in determining the character of the coöperation or "morale," particularly if the individuals have not been well prepared for coöperation and need assistance in making an adjustment.

Like many such words, the word "morale" jumps into prominence when that to which it refers is either conspicuously absent or conspicuously present (for example, France in May 1940, England in 1941). Like the state of our health, it becomes most important when we lose it. "Morale," in its everyday manifestations, is likely to be ignored and disregarded. Many aspects of our everyday existence have this character; that is, they include factors which we take for granted and whose important functions we therefore fail to recognize until they are drastically changed or disappear. We mentioned this point in connection with our discussion of routine ways of behaving which bind us in collaborative effort. Only when we lose a customary way of doing things, only when we are threatened with the loss of our customary way of life, do we realize its importance to us. Nothing makes us feel more insecure, uncertain, apprehensive, and demoralized than to have our routine ways of behavior too quickly and too arbitrarily interfered with.

In Chapter IV, we had something to say on this subject when we compared the basic assumptions of a primitive type of social organization with the basic assumptions of our modern industrial civilization. The primitive assumes that all is well if he preserves his traditional ways of doing things; the economic problems will more or less take care of themselves. Modern man assumes that all is well if the technical and economic factors determining the production and distribution of goods are taken care of; the social codes of human association will more or less take care of themselves. And then, perhaps indulging somewhat in oversimplification, we concluded, "As a result we have the goods, but the natives have the morale."

Let us continue with the analogy between health and morale. In medicine, for example, the physician is not interested in health or sickness in general; he is interested in diagnosing and treating particular organic situations. He has no treatment for disease in general; his treatment follows rather than precedes diagnosis; it is specific to the diagnosis of the particular organic ailment and the personal situation of the patient. Why then should we think that because there is a word "morale" there is one thing to which it refers? Why then should we think that we can treat something in general before we know in particular the many different states and kinds of equilibrium — personal and social — to which this word may refer? In medicine such an attitude has long since disappeared. To those who still think that certain herbs can cure all illnesses, a certain unfavorable label is now applied. But there are many of us who still think that certain magical words, regardless of the particular situations to which they are applied, can produce morale. It may be well to remember that to people who have lost their traditional ways of work, who are living in a social void, these symbols may have lost their customary significance. They may cease to motivate, except in a direction we do not want.

Although the physician has no specific remedies for sickness in general, he does have a simple and useful way of thinking about the physical organism. He conceives of the organism as being made up of parts which are interrelated and interdependent. That is, he conceives of the physical organism in relation to its physical environment as a physicochemical system — something which must be considered as a whole because each part bears a relation of interdependence to every other part. These parts are in a relation of equilibrium such that a slight change in one part produces changes in other parts of the system tending toward restoring the equilibrium. In this sense he does conceive of ill health or sickness as an organic unbalance of some kind; but the nature of the particular unbalance, the particular interferences making for unbalance, and hence the particular treatment required to restore the balance, can be determined only by a study of the concrete case of the particular patient. And this is where the skill and experience of the physician come in. As a result, the treatment, far from being the same, is different for different patients even though the symptoms may be very similar. In the case of patient *A*, this point of view leads to a diagnosis which prescribes treatment *A*; in the case of patient *B*, it leads to a diagnosis which prescribes treatment *B*.

It is our thesis that what physical health is to a physical organism, morale is to a coöperative system. Lack of morale, like lack of health, cannot often be reduced to some one simple cause. Just as problems relating to health require a simple and useful way of thinking about the physical organism as a physicochemical system, so an understanding of problems relating to morale requires a simple and useful way of thinking about human beings in their associations with one another as a social system.

From this point of view, the problems of morale in a business organization break down into two parts: (1) the daily problems of maintaining internal equilibrium within the organization, that is, maintaining that kind of social organization in which individuals and groups through working together can obtain human satisfactions that will make them willing to contribute their services to the economic objective of coöperation; and (2) the daily problems of diagnosing possible sources of interference, of locating sore spots, of liquidating human tensions and strains among individuals and groups, of helping people to orient themselves to their work groups, of spotting blockages in the channels of communication. These are the two "human controls" exercised by the administrator.

Maintaining internal equilibrium within the social organization of the plant involves keeping the channels of communication free and clear so that orders are transmitted downward without distortion and so that relevant information regarding situations at the work level is transmitted upward without distortion to those levels at which it can be best made use of. This involves getting the bottom of the organization to understand the economic objectives of the top; it also means getting the top of the organization to understand the feelings and sentiments of the bottom. It involves moving people about in the organization — transferring, upgrading, downgrading, promoting, demoting, placing, and selecting — in a manner that will be in accordance with the social values of the human situation and hence in a manner that will preserve morale.[5]

This is the problem of morale in its everyday manifestation. In this context morale is not a quality attaching to an individual or to a group; it is a dynamic relation of equilibrium between individuals and the organization they serve. To call the word "morale" into being when coöperation has ceased to exist in fact is too late. It should also be noted that in this context the administrator is the guardian or preserver of morale through the function of maintaining a condition of equilibrium which will preserve the social values existing in the coöperative system. Only in this sense does he have "authority."

To preserve the social values existing in the coöperative system, the administrator needs skills of diagnosing human situations. To expect him to exercise effective control, to maintain authority, to obtain loyalty and confidence without such skills is to ask him to stay in a horse-and-buggy stage with regard to this aspect of his job when the remainder of it has long since become streamlined. It is our contention that these skills no longer need to remain intuitive and personal. They can be clearly formulated and applied. The introduction of these skills in our modern business organizations is the challenge of our times. There is a need for the explicit recognition and systematic application of a specialty which is addressing itself to the adequate diagnosis and understanding of the actual human situations — both individual and group — within the business organization. This is the intelligent exercising of control. It is addressing ourselves to concrete situations and

[5] For a systematic treatment, see Roethlisberger and Dickson, *Management and the Worker*, chapter xxv.

finding out what are present here and now in the form of interferences and what can be done here and now to correct them.

This job needs to be done continuously, even daily. To expect that human problems can be fixed up once and for all is absurd. No matter how well they are handled, local unbalances will arise. They need to be continuously attended to. To expect loyalty and confidence and willingness to contribute their services from people whose feelings of personal integrity have been damaged — no matter how unwittingly — is to ask for the moon.

It is our hope that in time, through the practice of these skills, the word "morale" will drop from the vocabulary of administrators and their staff specialists concerned with human situations, just as the word "health" has dropped from the terminology of medicine. In its place will be substituted effective classifications of human situations and skillful methods of treating them. In this modern organization it will become just as old-fashioned to ask, "What is the state of morale of your department?" as for a physician to go into a modern hospital and ask, "What is the state of health of our patients?" In its place will be asked, "What are the particular human situations in your department, and how are you handling them?" This will be the exercise of "control" by understanding and not by ritualistic, verbal practices which address themselves to human nature in general, but not to *particular* human beings in *particular* places with *particular* feelings and sentiments for which they need concrete social expression.

NOTE

Chapter II was given as an address before the New England Conference on National Defense, Boston, April 6, 1941. Chapter III was an address to Professor Cabot's Business Executives' Group, Boston, February 9, 1936; it was subsequently published in *Business and Modern Society*, edited by Malcolm P. McNair and Howard T. Lewis (Harvard University Press, 1938). Chapter IV was an address to Professor Cabot's Business Executives' Group, Boston, December 5, 1936; Chapter V, an address to the same group, December 22, 1937, published under the title "Social Behavior in Industry" in the *Harvard Business Review* (vol. XVI, no. 4, Summer, 1938) and reprinted here by permission; Chapter VI, an address to the same group, March 10, 1940, the latter half slightly expanded for the purposes of the present book; Chapter VII, an address to the same group, December 11, 1938, revised for the purposes of the present book.

The Foreword by Elton Mayo was given as an address before the New England Conference on National Defense, Boston, April 5, 1941.

Bei Fragen zur Produktsicherheit wenden Sie sich bitte an:
If you have any questions regarding product safety,
please contact:

Walter de Gruyter GmbH
Genthiner Straße 13
10785 Berlin
productsafety@degruyterbrill.com